FRANK
LAMPARD

World Cup Heroes.

FRANK LAMPARD

Douglas Thompson

JOHN BLAKE

Published by John Blake Publishing Ltd,
3 Bramber Court, 2 Bramber Road,
London W14 9PB, England

www.johnblakepublishing.co.uk

This edition published in paperback in 2010

ISBN: 978 1 84358 172 7

British Library Cataloguing-in-Publication Data:

A catalogue record for this book is available from the British Library.

Design by www.envydesign.co.uk

Printed and bound in Great Britain by CPI Bookmarque, Croydon, CR0 4TD

1 3 5 7 9 10 8 6 4 2

Papers used by John Blake Publishing are natural, recyclable products
made from wood grown in sustainable forests. The manufacturing processes
conform to the environmental regulations of the country of origin.

Pictures reproduced by kind permission of Cleva, All Action, Empics,
Getty Images and Mirrorpix

1

For much of the past century, London's East End was patrolled by the valiant and the villains, but the one thing that everyone agreed on was that the family always came first.

Frank Lampard's traditional upbringing, which had novel and unorthodox aspects, as he was to find out, was very much meat and potatoes. Dad was playing football or down the Black Lion pub, sipping lager with Bobby Moore and the lads. His mother Pat would be in the kitchen, and sometimes Harry Redknapp, Uncle 'Arry, (the husband of Pat's sister, Sandra), would pop in and talk about the future of West Ham and, after another bottle of red wine, he'd predict the futures of the cousins, Frank Junior and his own son, Jamie Redknapp.

Harry's local pub was the Blind Beggar in London's Whitechapel, where George Cornwell was murdered by the Kray twins. It was that sort of topsy-turvy world: money, politics and football. What's changed?

* * *

Frank Lampard Senior began his career at West Ham in 1967 with World Cup heroes like Bobby Moore, Martin Peters and Geoff Hurst. He made 633 appearances for the club and played twice for his country.

He became part of East End football folklore when he played in West Ham's 1980 FA Cup Final win over Arsenal.

That victory only became possible because of his sudden appearance in Everton's penalty area in the semi-final replay, when he scored with a back-post header after a cross from Trevor Brooking. (OK, it was the defender's dance around the corner flag that contributed as much to his legend as the goal.) But the one man he couldn't handle with a football was Harry Redknapp. A clever player, he bamboozled Frank Senior when they had a kick-around game on the Isle of Sheppey in the late 1970s. Frank Senior had just been picked to play for England.

Young Frank Junior and his sisters Claire and Natalie grew up hearing football stories, the dramas, the near misses, the mistaken referees, the boneheaded management and manager, and the egotistical players, the temperamental ones and the class acts; they lived the ups and downs of the glories and defeats.

Every Saturday, three hours before home games, Frank Senior would eat a steak. Before 6pm, around the time *Dr Who* started and they'd finished hearing the football results on the radio or television, he'd be in the Black Lion with Bobby Moore and the lads. And that routine didn't vary too much between 1967 and 1985.

'Win or lose always on the booze' was Bobby Moore's saying, and one that was often repeated by Harry. Harry Redknapp made 149 League appearances for West Ham before moving to Bournemouth in 1972. His life at Upton Park, like many of his team-mates, revolved around the game, betting on cards and the dogs, and enjoying a drink.

Frank Lampard Senior was a players' player from the word go. He just frowns at any suggestion that he might have played for any other club than West Ham: 'Claret and blue flows through my blood.'

In 1971, Sir Alf Ramsey gave official recognition to his talents by naming him in the England Under-23 side.

Originally spotted by the legendary scout Wally St Pier, the strong (5ft 10in, 12 stone in his day) defender had suffered a severe leg break in 1967 and endured a long and painful recovery. But for that he might have won more England caps.

'If I have one regret, it is not winning more caps for my country. The moment I walked out at Wembley in an England shirt was the proudest of my life. I've still got the shirt tucked away somewhere – it is a trophy they can never take away.

'The feeling of walking out in front of such a huge crowd is indescribable and one that stays with you forever. Things change when you represent your country. Wherever you go, fans want to shake your hand and talk to you...'

Frank Senior took out insurance for his family's future by investing in the haulage business, a pub and a dry cleaners in Canning Town, but his priority was always football. He had arrived at West Ham just as the old guard of Moore (who played 642 times for West Ham from 1958–74), Hurst and Peters was beginning to change.

But as his own career matured, his thoughts began to turn to his son.

'I just felt I had done all right and that football had given me a chance to experience things and places I wouldn't have been able to do otherwise in life. I thought that if Frank was good enough to come through as a player then the rewards were there. I don't think I am any different from any other dad in that I am my son's worst critic and yet his biggest punter. It's not been easy for him to make the grade, as he has had to put up with the sniping behind his back.

'I always stressed to Frank that he should be more of an attacking player, because it is always the midfielders and the strikers who get all the accolades. When I was a kid Bobby Moore was one of my heroes. The way I played, the way I thought about the game was from him.'

Frank Senior and Bobby Moore had a relationship which resonates in the career of Frank Lampard Junior. Frank is not coy about encouraging or praising his team-mates. Sure, he wants to score the goals – that's where the glory is – but the essential lesson he has learned is that you are nothing without the club. You have to earn your place and work to keep it. If you are on the bench, you might as well be in the Falkland Islands. Bobby Moore, for all the accolades, knew that. 'When youngsters join a club they copy the pros. If they are copying pros who arrive in the morning, sit down and read the paper and dash off as soon as training ends, that's how they are going to grow up.

'They should learn the good habits that were instilled in us at West Ham. Everybody wants players who are prepared to work that little bit extra.'

2

Young Frank Lampard had no need to use football as a path out of inner-city poverty or problems. His father's financial diligence had taken care of that.

'Dad had to wait a long time to get a son. I have two older sisters and, when I was born, I reckon he just threw the ball at my feet and said, "That's a football – kick it."

'I had a lot of football knowledge pumped into me from an early age, but the other side of the coin of having a father with his record is that you tend to be very self-critical.'

His father says he took to football 'like a duck to water', but he'd seen other youngsters' careers collapse, so he arranged for his son to have a private education. At Brentwood School, Frank Junior applied himself as much to books as to sport; he did exceptionally well at cricket and, as a very young lad, was soon playing in youth soccer teams. He went from kicking a ball around the garden at the age of six to Sunday morning games with kids two and, sometimes, even four years older than himself.

'Frank never came to me and said he wanted to be a professional, it was one of those situations that just developed over the years. As an ex-pro, the first thing you want is for a son to kick a ball. His enjoyment was so obvious. Give him a ball and he would carry on until he dropped.'

Frank went on to play for Heath Park at youth level but

the parents of the other players complained that he was only in the team because of who his father was. It is one thing to take all the sticks and stones going at professional level, but suffering the smugness and stupidity of the small-minded needs anger management. Frank Junior does it his way: 'I still feel that I am proving these people wrong whenever I go on to the field.'

And there were always pressures. 'Dad doesn't often show his feelings. He manages to get his point over pretty well. He's my biggest fan and biggest critic. He always will be. We've had countless rows and arguments, but afterwards I usually realise he's right ... The rest of the family, my sisters, my mum, have also been a support. It was always football, football, football at home and sometimes it would do your head in. I'd go and talk to mum just to get a release.'

When Frank Junior was excelling at cricket at Brentwood School, there was much talk of him becoming a professional cricketer, even of playing for England. He was that good. There were moves by coaches from the South of England Independent Schools to enlist young Frank as a future cricket star and it led to a front room talk between mum and dad.

'Football or cricket?' Frank Senior was asked.

'The boy can do what he likes,' he said, and then he walked out the door. About 30 seconds ticked away. Then the door opened and Frank Senior's head reappeared and, with a smile, he added, 'He can do what he likes as long as he plays football...', The family business.

Frank Senior was eight years old when he first started kicking a ball at Upton Park and 15 when he was being coached by the legendary Ron Greenwood ('the only one great coach', according to Harry Redknapp) at West Ham. His son signed his Youth Training Scheme papers with the club, ignoring the temptations of Arsenal and Spurs, on 1 August 1992, when he was close to the same age.

'I wasn't even working with West Ham when he decided to sign his YTS forms – he made the final decision to play for the Hammers,' said Frank Senior, adding, 'He was very lucky. A lot of my old mates from Canning Town still watch West Ham from the terraces. All of them were football nuts, just like me, desperate to play for the local side. I managed to get there.

'I felt I was representing them, those blokes who wanted to be out there on the pitch busting a gut for their club. The same thing happened to Frank. A lot of his pals stood on the same terraces doing exactly the same as my mates. Frank realised he was their standard bearer – he wanted to give them his best, just as I wanted to give them mine.'

Frank Junior revealed, 'I nearly went to Spurs but in the end I chose West Ham. It was the club I supported, after all.'

There had been some famous graduates from the West Ham Academy, most memorably the 1966 World Cup trio of Bobby Moore, Geoff Hurst and Martin Peters, and now Frank Junior, Rio Ferdinand and Trevor Sinclair, nearly four decades on, were getting the headlines.

Harry Redknapp has always made a great deal of how 'his' boys flourished at West Ham. In 1994, when he took over as manager, he brought back a former graduate, Frank Lampard Senior. The former West Ham full-back had been working part-time with the club, scouting and coaching.

His property business was so successful that it cost him financially to return to full-time football as West Ham's assistant manager. 'I had a lot of things to consider, but the lure of the job proved too much. If it had been anyone else but Harry and any other club but West Ham I wouldn't have done it. When I did, I couldn't wait to get there every morning and get the tracksuit on.'

But, with two Frank Lampards at West Ham, the accusations of nepotism intensified. Being the man he is, however, Frank Lampard Senior was going out of his way not to do his son any favours. As always the advice was, 'Let your football do the talking.' And he told him about footballing fame. 'All players have to suffer a bit of abuse at times, even the great Bobby Moore. It's how you deal with it that's important. I always found it a little ironic, because young Frank was representing the fans on the pitch. He was claret and blue right through.'

Frank was bright, he had dealt capably with his education and his future was clear to him: all he had to do was play football to the best of his ability, to learn and improve. He had an extraordinary support system. Yet the fans were telling him to stuff it and far worse. But he stuck to his guns.

'Part of the reason for my progress is that I made a conscious effort when I was 16 or 17 that I needed to add more to my game. I could always hit the pass and be neat and tidy. But that extra bit, of scoring goals and being box to box, adds more to your game. You realise you need that if you are going to be a complete player. I think it was probably dad as well who drummed that into me.'

But many of the fans believed his progress, his elevation, was only because of his father. And once you pick up that particular stick it tends to grow branches. When he made his first appearance as a substitute for West Ham in January 1996, a section of the Upton Park crowd started booing. It was hurtful and menacing and upset many of those present. What young lad needed this treatment?

Certainly, the professionals saw how unpleasant it was. The affable Scot Gordon Strachan, then the Coventry player-manager, who had brought himself on at the same time as Frank, put his arm round him to console him. Frank was just 17 years old and it has to rank as one of the cruellest introductions any player has undergone. Yet his father emphasised, probably more optimistically than realistically, 'He never let it worry him. He showed them what a terrific temperament he has got. He took it in his stride. They thought it was nepotism, but it wasn't. Harry and I knew what he could do. He was there on merit. Frank had made a few appearances as a substitute in his first season, coming on in the last five minutes. A lot of the punters thought we were just trying to sort him out with appearance money bonuses.'

Frank admitted, 'I was young when I started getting all the remarks. It is hard for someone that age to take it because you have no experience. You try to ignore the criticism, but that little bit can hurt and it did. There were boos and comments and that was disappointing. The reception I got never made me think I should leave; I was always West Ham from the start.

'I'd hear the effing and blinding from the terraces. Both home and away. "You're not as good as your old man." "You're not fit to lace his boots." It hurt. It piled on the pressure. I worked twice as hard to prove myself to the manager who picked the team, and the fans. It's not any fun but it makes you stronger; you want to prove them so wrong. I suppose the advantage from a young age is that people recognise you, and you stand out because of your name.

'It's tough for any player who is a victim of the boo-boys. It knocks your confidence and gets under your skin. I honestly don't think people realise what damage they can do to a player. But I know you have to be able to take it on the chin in this game and be big enough to take the flak and come back for more if necessary.'

3

In the mid-1990s, Harry Redknapp and Frank Lampard Senior were nurturing a group of young players and Frank Junior was starting to graduate from schoolboy player. There was also Rio Ferdinand who, as a 14-year-old, would go round to tea at the Lampards, while Trevor Sinclair and Joe Cole were waiting in the wings.

West Ham won the FA Youth Cup and Frank, Rio and Joe Cole were seen as pivotal to English football's future. Cole in those days was anointed as the player who would wear Paul Gascoigne's crown, the most exciting prodigy since Gazza first fizzed and whizzed huge bursts of energy into Newcastle.

Rio had advertised himself as an attacking midfielder. In the second leg of a Youth Cup final against Chelsea, playing just behind the main striker, he scored one, made two and, though only a schoolboy in a fully fledged youth team, announced his self-belief by successfully taking one of the penalties in the shoot-out.

'That was when I first realised he was top class,' recalled his friend Frank Junior adding, 'He was brilliant that night. From that moment, the question changed from "can he play?" to "where should he play?"'

Frank learned. He watched Rio make the game come to him rather than the other way round, which his father had always told him was one of Bobby Moore's great skills.

Of course, at West Ham in the late 1990s, Harry Redknapp reckoned he had the nucleus of a seriously good football side with Rio, Joe and Frank always being compared to Moore, Hurst and Peters, the Class of '66. It was very interesting but, as with many things in football, just a theory. What Frank Lampard Junior wanted was action. He got his first full taste of it in August 1996, at the beginning of the season. Then all the talk post Euro '96 was about foreign players: spending in the Premier League had swelled to an unprecedented £90 million. Nearly a decade later it looks like small change. Then, it emphasised that foreign was best, or thought to be so.

Harry Redknapp's West Ham, known as 'The United Nations', got a different look with the introduction of old-fashioned East End local boy Frank Lampard for the 17 August 1996 match against Arsenal (which the Gunners won 2–0).

Redknapp admitted at the time, 'Over the last couple of seasons I have been as responsible as anyone for going abroad to buy players. For me the reason was simple. We couldn't afford the prices being asked at home for the quality needed. But nothing gives me greater pleasure than seeing one of our lads come up through the ranks, and it could be a dream for me if in a few years we could field a team full of locals.

'The trouble has been that the club which used to pride itself on producing its own players had a barren patch. Last season we saw Danny Williamson make an impact and now young Frank has got his chance. I feel that this will be the first of many, many games at the club for him.

'He is an outstanding prospect who can go a long way. The same goes for Rio Ferdinand, who would have played had Slaven Bilic not declared himself fit. Frank and Rio are the first of a very healthy crop.'

Yet it was Frank who had spent much of the 1996–97 season on the substitutes' bench while Rio earned the plaudits. Frank says Rio's swift advancement inspired him. 'The fact that Rio got so much praise helped me too. Rio and I went about everywhere together and I didn't begrudge him a thing. When Rio broke in he got loads of accolades and it was all totally deserved. Maybe that was the little jolt I needed. I saw Rio getting all the praise and getting in the side and I thought, "I want that". And I went for it. I pulled my finger out and I came back determined to get my own thing going.'

In West Ham's 1997–98 season, Frank just wanted his chance, which he got on the opening game of the season on 9 August 1997, the hottest day of the year. Frank also sizzled, against Barnsley.

West Ham had won just once on the opening day of the season in their past 10 attempts. It didn't look good at half time, as they went in trailing by one goal. Then John Hartson nodded the equaliser and, with a quarter of an hour remaining, Frank scored West Ham's winner. He flicked the ball past David Watson 30 seconds after having come on as a substitute. The headline? 'Phew, what a scorcher!'

Frank kept driving forward but there was no sudden leap to first-team fame. It has been that way with Frank: first Rio got the attention and later, in Euro 2004, Wayne Rooney, as Frank gradually moved his game up a gear. He has always been in the business of building dreams, putting down foundations for that climb to the very top. But there were distractions and temptations. He was only a teenager.

* * *

Footballers were more sought after than rock stars, and Frank and the other lads from the Academy were millionaires in the making, magnets for all the glamour and glitter that goes with the money.

Frank and Rio – 'best pals since they had their backsides hanging out of their trousers', according to Harry Redknapp' – got England glory at the same time, albeit at different levels. Frank made his debut in the England Under-21 team against Greece in Crete on 13 November 1997. The 6ft 3in Rio, five months his junior (born in London's Peckham on 7 November 1978), made his first full England appearance in a friendly against Cameroon at Wembley the same month. In the previous weeks they had both run into trouble with the bosses of their England squads for drinking.

Rio began his schoolboy football as a centre-forward. He later moved to central midfield and was playing for Eltham Town Under-14s when he attracted the West Ham scouts. At 14 he was signed as a schoolboy and, two years later, stayed on, despite attracting interest from both Middlesbrough and Chelsea.

On a two-year YTS contract (earning £30 a week), he and Frank helped the club's youth team win the South-East Counties League with a record number of points. Harry Redknapp signed Rio on his first professional contract when he turned 17.

Redknapp had sent Frank to Swansea on loan in October 1995, and a year later he followed up his 'character-building' method by dispatching Rio to Bournemouth for eight weeks from November 1996. It paid dividends for the two lads: if Frank was the new Martin Peters, then Rio's performances urged comparisons with Bobby Moore.

They were both now earning fantastic wages for their age, and their lifestyles reflected their wealth. Glenn Hoddle was the England manager and he called up Rio for a World

Cup qualifier against Moldova in 1997. Rio went out to celebrate. After an evening drinking with friends, he was stopped as he was driving home and got a 12-month driving ban. He also missed the World Cup game, dropped from the senior squad. 'I understood why Glenn had no alternative but to leave me out of the team. At the time I was worried that he would never pick me again,' he confessed.

What he said next reminds us that these big, strong lads are just that: lads. 'But I think I was more scared about telling my mum. It took me a whole day to pluck up the courage to break the news to her. In the end she was really understanding and helped me sort everything out with the police. I knew I had made a stupid mistake and I learned from it.'

Frank and Rio were included in the squad for the first leg of the European Championship play-off against Greece in Crete on 13 November. Rio moved up to the seniors, but for Frank it was his start on the international ladder; soon he would be captain of the Under-21s.

Around the same time, footballing life was looking grand at Upton Park. It's hard to pick a breakthrough moment, but the Coca-Cola Cup, when West Ham took down Walsall 4–2 on 19 November 1997, was when Frank clearly took on the responsibility to score goals as well as make them.

His hat-trick made headlines. Matt Dickinson reported in *The Times* on 27 November 1997, 'West Ham United can still claim to be an academy and their latest young talent, Frank Lampard, displayed his burgeoning talents last night with an impressive hat-trick that spared his team from some anxious moments in a treacherous Coca-Cola Cup fourth-round tie.'

Redknapp said, 'I get immense pleasure that we are starting to get some kids coming through. It's been almost

10 years since we produced players of any real note and now I have Frank and Rio coming through, and there are more behind them.

'I am especially pleased for Frank because, let's be honest, when he first got in the side he did not get a very good reception, which we were all disappointed about. People maybe thought something stupid like he was getting his chance because his old man is here, but I always knew he would be a good player and now he is getting stronger.'

For Frank, it was the beginning of his seduction of the Upton Park sceptics, although he revealed, 'Dad didn't even say much then. But I could tell by the look on his face that he was pleased with me. I've always tried to follow dad's example, the way he conducts himself at the club and away from it. I hope I made him proud. It wasn't easy with my dad at the club and there was a time when I thought it might be better if I went somewhere else, but I got over that.

'With the fans I felt that I was winning them over with each performance. But you were on audition all the time. It was pressure. It drove me on.'

4

Frank Lampard was like a young stallion: he just couldn't wait to be set free. He kept working. He kept improving. He kept waiting to be noticed. He was playing game after game for the England Under-21 team and was now its captain. He had proved himself to almost everybody; when he touched the ball there were cheers, not jeers, from the West Ham fans.

Yet, it was only in 1998 that the official West Ham programme reflected the wishes of their superstar-in-waiting. Frank Lampard would no longer be 'Junior'. From now on he'd be distinguished from his father because the latter would be called 'Senior'. For Frank it was like getting the keys to the family car. He was trusted on his own.

'I realised I had to get rid of that tag, otherwise it was going to plague my career at West Ham. It always upset me as a teenager. I always wanted to do my best and I worked hard at it, but there were such big sections of people out there not willing to give me a fair chance. I suppose I did feel persecuted. Maybe since I lost the Junior bit it's been easier for me to get on and play my own game.'

The England manager Glenn Hoddle, had promised that 'youth' would get a chance for England's friendly against the Czech Republic on 18 November 1998. So, playing against Chelsea 10 days earlier felt very much like a first-team audition, almost a dress rehearsal. Hoddle was also aware of what a firm favourite Frank had become at West Ham.

That was emphasised when many of the West Ham faithful turned out to watch him captain the Under-21s in east London against Bulgaria. He received a huge reception and scored the winner; the highlight of his England Under-21 career. The chance of grown-up international glory was around the corner. Or so it seemed. He'd watched Michael Owen and friends like Rio and Kieron Dyer graduate from the Under-21s, but not for him this time. He was severely disappointed, having performed so well for the Under-21s in the previous two matches, but he did not sulk. He vowed to get his head down and work even harder.

The rejection appeared to fire Frank on. Which is why his call-up to the England team in April 1999 was all the more gratifying for him. He'd had his disappointments in World Cup year 1998; he'd made the 'B' team for a warm-up game against Chile, but that wasn't the real thing. So when the fax arrived at Upton Park telling him that Kevin Keegan, now the England boss, had picked him for the squad to face Hungary in Budapest, it was a moment of celebration. But there were the old doubts. His dad had once been in the Under-23 squad with Keegan. Would there be criticism? Then he told himself, 'My dad doesn't pick the England team.'

When Frank flew off to Budapest, Harry Redknapp took pleasure in saying, 'When I first saw Frank as a kid I knew he could become a player, but now he's got belief in himself as well. I remember when we gave him and Rio their debuts, I said then they could go all the way and nobody can say he doesn't deserve his chance.'

But he didn't get it. He made it as far as the bench. Commentators wondered if he was held back because of his importance to the Under-21s. At that time Frank refused to go near that argument and still does. He'd been part of the young England team that beat Poland 5–0, regarded as the best performance ever by an Under-21 side. He'd been an inspirational captain.

And now Frank was wanted by West Ham's rivals. Spurs and Aston Villa were both keen to sign him; he was rated at around £7 million. Early in 1999 Spurs made a £4 million bid and, after that was rejected, were increasing the money.

Harry Redknapp was furious about attempts to kidnap 'his' boys. At the time he fumed, 'We're not looking to sell our young players. Why should we? It annoys me when I hear Tottenham are going to sign Frank Lampard. Why should he go to Spurs? Why shouldn't we think big. We're not second-class citizens. If we sell the Frank Lampards, Rio Ferdinands and the Joe Coles of this world, we will never be up there with the big boys.'

So Frank was still with West Ham when the England dream finally did become reality. By then he'd played 14 games for the Under-21s and scored seven goals. His goal ratio was as good as any front-line striker. Kevin Keegan brought him into the squad to play Belgium (England won 2–1 at Sunderland) on 10 October 1999.

What Frank had wanted most of all was a chance to prove himself not just for West Ham but for England. Now he was getting the chance. All the scouts knew he was a quick learner, a potential winner, and that potent mix of a midfielder who could get forward and score goals.

'Frank was always a potential World Cup-winning player for England,' said a seasoned television pundit in 2005 on his breakthrough days. He added, 'He'll be captain in 2006 – he's got that sort of solid quality and background. If there's a chance of getting back the World Cup in 2006 – and wouldn't that be magical? – you have to believe in football and voodoo and every other sort of religion. And if there's any chance at all then Frank will be there... he's the leader of a gang that might just do it. The East End boys did it before. And they're not afraid of anything. Even voodoo. They might have invented that...'

5

Frank was winning hearts. He was a pin-up. The young lads of West Ham were making a name for themselves around town. There were parties and late nights, but not to their game's detriment. They were young enough and fit enough. Especially for their growing army of female fans. Frank and Rio were quite a duo on the dating circuit.

Frank was now part of a world of which television and series like *Footballers' Wives* only nicked the surface. One of the circuit said, 'I know of one player who spent £26,000 a month on clothes, watches and jewellery. And another who has 17 wardrobes stuffed with unworn designer clothes. Despite their high income, these players can end up thousands of pounds overdrawn at the end of the month. I know it doesn't seem possible.

'They take their cue from people like David Beckham, but they don't earn David's money. Frank's the real thing – he will earn that sort of money one day and without having to marry a pop star. He and Rio used to joke that they weren't going to be Spice boys. And when he gets the money, you know it's not going to go on bling. Frank's from the land of diamond geezers – he's not the platinum jewellery sort. You can bet it will go in property. I think Frank's old man has sold more flats than he's kicked footballs. When his mobile goes, it's usually another punter wanting to buy. They're clever boys.'

And Gabby Yorath would not have been interested if Frank was not a serious person. She was hosting ITV's *On The Ball* when she met him. It was the roundabout world of football. Rio was dating Kirsty Gallagher and she introduced his friend to her friend. Frank and Gabby were soon seeing much of each other, especially in Richmond, Surrey.

Gabby, daughter of former Welsh football star Terry, was a footballers' and fans' fantasy. The beautiful game's number-one television sex symbol. And who did she fancy? She'd tried to avoid footballers but Frank lured her in. According to one television pundit, she saw Frank as level-headed and was attracted to him, and he was very smitten. The romantic potion worked... for a time.

At the same time as Frank became a more and more integral part of the West Ham team, there was an increased need for magic of any variety at Upton Park. They'd finished in the top half of the Premiership for a couple of years, but it was a struggle. What makes a good club? Good management. What makes good management? Good players.

The magic, always the magic, is knowing how to play and handle them. But in the financial world of football – and Frank was to find himself at the luxury end – it's all about trade offs and compromise.

With Rio, Frank, Joe Cole, Michael Carrick and Trevor Sinclair, Harry Redknapp had a multi-million-pound fund of assets. But club chairman Terry Brown had the key to the safe. In the summer of 1999, Frank had resisted attempts by Brown to contract him to West Ham for the foreseeable future.

There were also lots of rumours, mainly surrounding Rio's future. But the word was West Ham would never sell Rio. That might have been because Harry Redknapp set the price too high. Whatever the reason, it was what Frank wanted to believe – and to hear. Fiercely ambitious, he knew he needed a winning club to prosper.

When Rio did sign and committed himself to West Ham in July 1999, his best friend did the same within 48 hours. Frank signed a £1-million-a-year deal set to run until 2005. He had seen Rio, Paolo Di Canio and Ian Wright do better in the pay stakes but was happier that he was getting close to what he thought he was worth. The fans who had given him such a hard time had been lobbying for him to be given everything he wanted to stay with the club. When he did, he vowed to himself that he'd help West Ham up the Premiership ladder and get himself a permanent spot in the England senior squad. Still the undisputed Under-21 captain, his call up against Belgium appeared very much a one-off.

But West Ham were not having the best of times. Yes, there were injuries, but something wasn't working for them. Frank was producing the driving football his team needed, but the goals were not multiplying as they should have done in their troubled season. Meanwhile, Terry Brown wanted to sell Rio to Leeds for £15 million. He told his manager, 'Look, Harry, the transfer system's falling apart, we'll never get this offer again.'

Harry Redknapp tried to talk Brown out of it. He said, 'Listen, they'll come back for more.'

(Pause.)

'And if not, Barcelona will buy him.'

(Silence.)

Then Harry added, 'For he's the best.'

The chairman could not fathom that. He argued, 'I can't see that.'

Three weeks later after that conversation at Upton Park, Leeds United manager David O'Leary made another offer for Rio. A bid of £18 million. If you look at it Harry's way, he had earned West Ham £1 million a week between the first and second offer.

Terry Brown told him, 'Harry, we've got to take it.'

Harry replied, 'Yeah, I see that.'

Seen from Rio's point of view, it was quite a leap forward, a rather large improvement, a multiple winning move for a player who'd been seriously happy not too long before to get £30 a week. The world-record £18 million deal, a five-and-a-half-year contract worth £30,000 a week, now made him the world's most expensive defender.

Frank was confused. He complained that he had signed his deal under false pretences. Rough words were exchanged, but he left it to his agent Steve Kuttner to say them. 'When we signed that deal we were promised West Ham would never sell any of their top players. Frank is deeply upset and feels he has been double-crossed by the club.'

Later, a calmer Frank said, 'I was told Rio wouldn't be sold and I was very upset when he was. I was surprised Rio went – and disappointed. I wish him well, and good luck to him, but I hope it doesn't send out the message that West Ham are only a selling club. That worries me.'

The seeds of discontent with West Ham were sown that winter. Within six months Frank got a telephone call from his mother Pat – and the West Ham story was over. Or just about.

6

'They've got the sack.' They're the words Frank's mother, Pat, rushed at him when he walked in the front door. His father and uncle were out of West Ham as of 9 May 2001. That's the day Harry Redknapp went into a meeting with his club's chairman Terry Brown. Redknapp had no idea that the confrontation would end with the dismantling of a pivotal part of the Hammers' history.

It began, like many disasters, with a small incident. Redknapp had agreed a new four-year contract with West Ham, but the club wanted more negotiations. He then did an interview with a fan magazine in which he made an offhand remark about the chairman's arithmetic in regard to the funds brought in by the sale of Rio Ferdinand to Leeds. Later Harry revealed, 'The chairman read it. He reads all the fanzines, looks at everything on the Internet. And he took the hump. So the following week after we'd beaten Southampton on the Saturday, I walked in to see about my contract and he says, "I'm not happy with you, Harry. I'm going to call it a day." I said, "OK. If that's how you feel. I've got two years left on my contract. You'd better make sure you sort me out." And that was that. Shame. I got on well with Terry Brown.'

Harry Redknapp's run at the club was all over, as was the Lampard legacy. At that moment it seemed Frank was going to join Rio at Leeds for a fee of around £12 million. Yet there were rumours of other offers from Aston Villa and Chelsea.

Everything was complicated. And, of course, much of it was personal – not just business.

Frank later recalled, 'My family were involved and the East End is strong on that. I just couldn't go on playing for West Ham. In these special circumstances I think that is both acceptable and understandable. We talked about it, the family and me, and I discussed the possibilities with my agent Steve Kuttner. I feel emotional and I guess I always will when I think about the sackings.'

Of his father and uncle he said, 'I know people say, "They'll be all right – they can look after themselves." But it's a shock no matter who it happens to. Pride is a big factor. To suddenly find yourself on the outside isn't easy.

'West Ham has been my life, basically, since I started training with them when I was eight years old. I have always been ambitious enough to want to move on to something bigger, a club where I could have a better chance of winning things. In a way they forced the decision, but I am sure it would have come anyway. It was a matter of time. I had been linked with Leeds and joining Rio at Elland Road and also with Aston Villa and Chelsea...'

Frank met with Claudio Ranieri at Stamford Bridge. He was impressed. He thought this was a terrific opening and he wanted to be part of it. The commentators said he'd join Rio at Leeds but he said, 'Everyone seemed to take it for granted because Rio was there, but they were wrong.

'When Rio left and I saw the success he was having I did feel a bit of what I suppose you could call professional jealousy. But just because something suited him didn't mean it would be the same for me. I wanted a big club and Chelsea are massive. It would have to be a club with ambition – and Chelsea are certainly that.'

Had he only known then of the upcoming Russian revolution. Yet you make your own luck by being brave. 'It was important to understand what the manager saw in me and expected from me. With Chelsea I would be surrounded by world-class players in a squad that was vastly experienced.

'Chelsea was the future...'

At which point it's quickly worth noting what happened to that crop of Upton Park graduates.

RIO FERDINAND (Manchester United) Joined Leeds from West Ham in November 2000 for a fee of £18 million. In July 2002 Manchester United paid £30 million to take him to Old Trafford.

GLEN JOHNSON (Liverpool) Was a West Ham first-team player for only 16 games before Chelsea signed him in July 2003 for £6 million. He soon became part of the England team. In 2007 he joined Portsmouth and then signed for Liverpool in 2009.

JOE COLE (Chelsea) Three weeks after Chelsea bought Glen Johnson, they paid £6.6 million for Joe, another England international. The skilful midfielder has flourished at Stamford Bridge, though his career has been hit by injury.

JERMAIN DEFOE (Tottenham) West Ham spotted his Jimmy Greaves-like touches when he was a teenager at Charlton and took him to Upton Park. Spurs signed him in February 2004, and again in 2009, when Harry Redknapp brought him back to White Hart Lane from Portsmouth.

MICHAEL CARRICK (Manchester United) West Ham sold him to Tottenham at the start of the 2004-05 season for £2.75 million. He began to forge a place for himself in the England midfield, and his control and passing earned him a move to Manchester United in 2006 for £18.6 million.

7

Frank completed his £11 million transfer across London from West Ham to Chelsea on 14 June 2001. The first great difference he noticed between West Ham and Chelsea was that of expectation. The management, the players, the fans all expected great things. 'We were talking at the start of the season about winning the League and the UEFA Cup, whereas at West Ham we may have said, "Can we get into Europe?"

'At Chelsea we didn't just hope to do well, but were expected to.' Frank was also impressed by his surroundings. 'The minute I walked into the stadium, the feel of the place got to me. What with the hotel on the site and the 45,000 capacity it feels like a big club. No disrespect to West Ham, but you're training with world-class players. Just watching and working with them, you can't help but learn. It feels like an honour to train with them.'

One of those exceptional and exciting players, Gianfranco Zola, recalls the arrival of Claudio Ranieri at Chelsea with some bemusement. Forget the football. There were some interesting cultural lessons to be learned as Zola, the one-time footballing partner of Diego Maradona, explained, 'When he first came, he handled the players like he would in Italy or Spain. I had to explain that in England he would have to be more accommodating. You cannot sit on players 24 hours a day. In Italy and Spain you control everything they do. In England it is different. You have to give them more space.'

But early in Frank's Chelsea career an incident occurred that suggested the players should be kept on a tighter, not a looser, rein.

In an indirect way the atrocities of 11 September 2001 also brought the world crashing down around Frank's ears. The day after the New York attacks, he went out on a drinking binge with some Chelsea team-mates and upset American visitors to London. The incidents of the day have been widely reported in the media.

After his dream transfer from West Ham to Chelsea, it was the last thing Frank Lampard needed. And what about his England hopes? On 18 November 2001, he told the forgiving Joe Lovejoy in the *Sunday Times*, 'There's a lot of things I could tell you about the whole day, but I'm not going into that. Let's just say that a lot of things people said happened didn't happen. None of the players who were involved are horrible people. We have just been painted that way, but it isn't like that.'

Later, in December 2004, he reflected on what had happened. He said he was happy to say 'sorry' and he admitted being 'loud'. But Chelsea fined the players involved two weeks' wages –£100,000 in total – and donated the money to the fund for bereaved families in America. The club's managing director Colin Hutchinson said, 'Their behaviour was totally out of order, but there is no way that the players went out, in any shape or form, to insult or abuse anyone.

Things got worse for Frank: he had a bad day at Spurs and was sent off on 16 September 2001. Just 12 days later he discovered that he had been left out of Sven-Goran Eriksson's plans for England's game against Greece. Eriksson, sensitive to the world situation, made it abundantly clear that players who stepped out of line would not be part of his World Cup plans. 'My players have to be professional. We are England. We are not a small country. We are one of the biggest in the world. That means we have to play well and have to conduct ourselves well and do everything well. You can't hope to win the World Cup in 2002 or 2006 if you accept anything less. I always make my selection decisions on footballing grounds. But, if a player isn't playing well or not doing well on or off the pitch, that has to do with football. All of us have a big responsibility if we want to be part of the England senior team. Millions of young people are looking at us as heroes when we are playing well. We must live up to that, whatever we do.'

Eriksson might have kicked Frank out of the World Cup qualifier against Greece, but his answerphone message gave him hope:. 'I'm leaving you out this time, but you're still in contention, still involved...'

In all the communications between them, Sven-Goran Eriksson never accused Frank of any wrongdoing. Yet, Frank paid his share of the fine and also achieved the dubious honour of becoming the first player dropped by England on non-footballing grounds since Rio Ferdinand was axed by Glenn Hoddle on the eve of the game with Moldova in September 1997, following his drink-drive conviction.

Frank, being Frank, then knuckled down. There was only one goal: the World Cup squad.

8

Frank and Chelsea dovetailed. The players, the club, the atmosphere. The magic happened. He was the first English signing for Claudio Ranieri and that was the beginning of a beautiful friendship.

Frank's message was clear. He had moved to Chelsea because he wanted to improve as a player and expand his horizons. The better those around him, the better he would become. He recalled, 'When I trained with England for the first time after Rio joined Leeds, I could see an improvement in him – not just as a player but as a person and in his strength of character. I was impressed by how much he had come on by playing in the Champions League and being made captain of Leeds. It adds another string to your bow.'

There were many around Frank then who could feel the burning ambition within him. Frank Lampard had a point to make. 'I had talks with West Ham about staying, but they didn't last very long. I had a good think about it, but I'd made up my mind. The first I heard of Chelsea's interest was from reading the paper. Chelsea want, and need, success and I am looking forward to testing myself against the best players in Europe. I think I proved myself at West Ham and I played for England while with them. But I'm sure playing in Europe will give me that extra edge.'

Sports columnist Jeff Powell, who reported on Frank Senior's career, said of the son, 'The interesting thing about young Frank is that he is one of the few players who plays every game, the same thing as players like his father did. He is considered to be a phenomenon because he just plays every match, whereas everybody else is getting rotated.

'They complain they can't play twice a week, while his father, and all the other guys at West Ham or wherever, from Bobby Moore downwards, were all playing every game, and a lot of those games were played on extremely heavy pitches with a great thumping old ball.

'This is what stopped them winning more World Cups. I think when we recently went to Japan, the most played player in the Eriksson team for the World Cup had 30-odd games in the season and a lot of those games were not full games. Well, there were no substitutes back in Frank Senior's day. Bobby Moore, in the season prior to leading us to the only World Cup we ever won, had played 63 games. You just got on with it. Young Frank is a bit of a throwback to that really. He's hard working and plays box to box and gets his goals and he plays every game, and very rarely comes off.'

Claudio Ranieri had joined Chelsea in September 2000, in the aftermath of the departure of Gianluca Vialli. The management turnover – Glen Hoddle, then Ruud Gullit – was, it seemed, a permanent way of life at Stamford Bridge where there had been nine managers in just 18 years.

Ranieri, surprised as anyone by the move, brought his own special skills and personality to the job. Of course he became known as 'the Tinkerman', for his frequent chopping and changing of the team, but he never had a chance to play any role in the departure, after seven seasons, of Gianfranco Zola from Chelsea to his Sardinian home and Cagilari. Ranieri was close to Zola, a player he described as 'the most loved Italian in England' and 'a vital leader in the dressing room'.

Ranieri then watched John Terry take on that role. Terry, who grew up on the same housing estate in Barking as Bobby Moore, was brought in from Chelsea's youth set-up by Ranieri, who astutely predicted that the tall, strong and most determined young man would develop into the Tony Adams' role for Chelsea – and England. He was impressed by the individual self-belief shown by Terry and by Frank, two of his favourite Chelsea 'sons'.

One clued-up commentator called the emergence of the duo 'Claudio Ranieri's greatest achievement' at Chelsea. Ranieri was certainly fond of them. 'They have a great spirit and that is so important, so vital in building confidence, in winning games. They show English strength and character. A team should always reflect the character of the nation.'

Ranieri was liked by the fans and the players, but did his affability blunt his killer instinct? The announcement of his move to London was given a deadpan précis in the Italian press: 'Claudio Ranieri was born in Rome in 1951. After an unspectacular playing career with Roma, he took up the coaching reins at Cagliari before moving on to Fiorentina, Valencia and Atletico Madrid. He quit Atletico in March 2000 and took over as manager at Chelsea later that summer.' But what was the reality?

The gregarious and good-natured Ranieri became someone the nation took to its heart, which was a surprise after his first reception at Chelsea, when thousands of fans shamelessly chanted the name of the club's previous manager, Gianluca Vialli, from the stands.

In two seasons at Valencia in Spain, Ranieri had laid the foundations for the club's run to the Champions League final. Then he stumbled. He accepted an offer from Atletico Madrid, where he clashed with Jesús Gil, a wealthy patron. Within a couple of months the club was on its way to relegation, in judicial administration and Gil was jailed. Ranieri resigned and spent the next six months out of the game kicking his well-heeled heels.

Then came the offer from Chelsea, which he accepted gratefully. He looked around for friends and found one, of course, in Zola, but also in Frank, who arrived at Chelsea a few months later. Ranieri liked Frank's attitude, which was basically that he would do whatever it took, however many hours of training, to be in the Chelsea team for every game. That's the way it worked.

It was no wonder Ranieri adopted him and, in turn, John Terry. His motivation was to create winners, but he was also aware that he was working for such an historic English football club. For Ranieri it was a marvellous adventure. In Italy, the newspapers reported how he had changed his hairstyle and his spectacles – he was a person always ready to wrap himself in a new country, a new identity. It was Ken Bates who gave him the job in September 2000, and the owner said then, 'The team are very disciplined and that comes from leadership from the top. When's the last time you heard him criticise a referee? When's the last time you heard him suggest he was temporarily blind? When's the last time you heard him slag off another opponent or manager?'

Ranieri did not control only himself. He was of the old school, a man who insisted on complete command of the dressing room and he was never put off by the thought of making himself unpopular. Jimmy Floyd Hasselbaink, during a rough time at Stamford Bridge, gave some sharp thoughts. 'I don't like it when, on the evening before a game, the manager storms into your hotel room and takes all the wires out of the television set because he's afraid you'll be watching it all night.'

'He was a very tough manager to work with,' said Irishman Damien Duff, adding, 'He made it really intense for us every single day in training. There was absolutely no let-up.'

But Frank admired the work ethic and thrived on it.

9

Claudio Ranieri made it clear to his Chelsea players, 'This is a new era for Chelsea. Whoever understands this rests with us. If they don't understand, I'm sorry. Instead of being with us they can rest.'

Frank, of course, got the message. But while Ranieri admired his play, there were elements of his game that drew the manager's criticism. 'He would follow a natural instinct that prompted him to get involved in attacking moves, and his sense of timing was perfect for it, but he made me cross sometimes because this exposed the midfield and, as I explained to him, if he was forever darting forward, he would never be able to count on the element of surprise, which, in his case, could be decisive.'

But by 2004 Ranieri admitted, 'With a string of phenomenal performances and goals, he forced me, gratifyingly, to play him in central midfield. Now my only problem was a different one: finding a way to rest him.'

His feelings towards Lampard were revealed further when he wrote following the Chelsea v Lazio game in the Champions League at Stamford Bridge on 22 October 2003, 'After eight minutes of the second half we had turned it around (from 0–1) with two genuine stunners from Lampard and Mutu. After the interval I saw the character of my team: a phenomenal Lampard (by now the norm) and Veron at his best since donning the blue of Chelsea.'

At home on 27 March 2004, when Chelsea beat Wolves 5–2, Ranieri said of his adopted 'son', 'A special day for Lampard – this was his 100th consecutive Premier League appearance. He scored one of his "super goals".' There was never any question as to whether Ranieri was a Frank Lampard superfan.

Throughout his reign, Ranieri never lost his concentration for the team – and much was going on around him. And beneath him. The foundations at Chelsea were being resoundingly shaken. Chelsea were in a financial quagmire and Ken Bates was floundering. The club needed new training facilities – a new start in life after nearly 100 years. Roman Abramovich bought the club in the summer of 2003, when Ranieri and his team were driving forward.

Actually, Ranieri was driving through France with his wife when he heard the news in a late night telephone call from Trevor Birch of Chelsea. Whatever emotions he felt, he should have been the happiest football manager on the planet. Four days later, he was sitting face to face with Abramovich, the new owner of Chelsea Football Club, who gave him more than £100 million to spend on buying a dream team.

Abramovich, quiet but determined, wanted a collection of stars who would pitch Chelsea into the stellar league of Manchester United and Real Madrid. Ranieri wanted a team. There was an underlying clash over stars and hard-working players but, for the moment, Ranieri was in. As he said earlier, he had no illusions about Abramovich's desires. 'I knew Roman didn't want me to drive the car, he wanted Schumacher. And he was looking for Schumacher.'

From then on there was much speculation. Would Sven-Goran Eriksson be in charge? Frank's friend, Eidur Gudjohnsen, recalled what went on after the takeover. 'As soon as I heard about the extent of Abramovich's wealth I knew there would be many new faces arriving before pre-season training. There was uncertainty among the existing players until Abramovich made it clear to us that he only wanted to add to the squad rather than get rid of people. From a personal point of view, it was difficult to sit and watch those early games from the bench, but when you're at a very big club – which is what all the new money made us – you just have to accept it.

'The other thing we had to get used to was Abramovich coming into the changing room after the game. He doesn't say too much; he just walks around and shakes hands with people. He never tried to interfere with team talks or tried to tell Claudio Ranieri what to do. That's not his job or why he's in there. I just think he wanted to show us that he was interested in the team, that he wanted us to succeed.

'The constant rumours that surrounded Claudio Ranieri, as to whether he would be leaving, didn't affect the players too much. We didn't really speak about it.'

It was Ranieri's dignity amid all the rumours about his future that endeared him to many. He also kept to his own rules: he picked hard-working players, like Frank, who might bond together. 'I wanted players with character. My idea was to create a group, because a team is a group and I wanted everybody to work together.'

Despite the guillotine hovering above him, Ranieri's strategy paid off. The big moment came when they recorded their first victory over Arsenal in six years on 6 April 2004. After Wayne Bridge's winning goal at Highbury, the Chelsea fans were chanting that Abramovich couldn't sack Ranieri now. Could he?

Chelsea were now the unexpected favourites to reach the Champions League final, something that had been achieved by only one English club, Manchester United, since 1985.

But there was such a whirlwind of rumours concerning Abramovich and his advisers that the Highbury win was seen by many as just a stay of execution for Ranieri. The manager also seemed to suspect as much, judging by his body language in the post-match interviews. He seemed very uncomfortable and frantically rubbed his nose.

On 17 March 2004, Ottmar Hitzfeld, the Bayern Munich coach, said he had been approached by Chelsea. And there were stories linking the club to two other coaches, Fabio Capello and Carlo Ancelotti.

Ranieri's tears flowed that night at Highbury and he made many lifelong friends that evening. Yes, he was emotional that Chelsea had beaten Arsenal against all the odds and stood on the cusp of an historic European Champions League final. But mostly his tears expressed relief and vindication that, after months of plotting to get rid of him, the then 52-year-old manager was not the 'dead man walking' that the pundits said he was. Not yet, anyway.

What had impressed everybody was the way that Ranieri had risen above the sustained efforts to undermine him. These came to a head about two weeks before the triumph at Highbury. It was leaked that Manchester United's former background mastermind Peter Kenyon, now Chelsea's chief executive, had invited the England coach, Sven-Goran Eriksson, for an afternoon tea meeting to discuss the possibility of him replacing Ranieri.

It was cat and mouse all over the front and back pages of the newspapers. The Swede's seriously active love life was of passing interest compared to his flirting between Chelsea and the national team. The Football Association was hoping – praying? – that they might go into the European Championships of 2004 with Eriksson's contract safely signed until 2008.

One clue was that Eriksson was more vocal than usual.

He needed to be. 'What? Because of a cup of tea? I'm amazed every time this comes up because I have a contract. Yes, I will be England manager after the European Championship because I don't have an offer to go elsewhere, absolutely, and that's the truth.'

There was an element of general outrage and the mounting uncertainty did not help Ranieri's or his team's situation. Frank and the lads could sense the effect it was having on all of them. And it was Ranieri's own success which led, arguably, to his failure to remain in west London.

Following their impressive win against Arsenal, they had to play AS Monaco in the Champions League semi-final on 20 April 2004. There was a great deal of pressure. Ranieri would have preferred to face Real Madrid. He was wary of Monaco and also upset by the news, whispered to him by one of football's Iagos, that Chelsea had been involved in meetings with people representing Jose Mourinho, then manager of FC Porto.

It made Ranieri much, much more determined to win. He changed, he tinkered mercilessly and he admits, 'That was my mistake.' He said that the news of the Chelsea-Mourinho connection had influenced his judgement. He had made the wrong choices. The name of Jose Mourinho haunted him.

Chelsea lost 3–1 and did not recover in the second leg. They were out of the Champions League. Ranieri was asked whether, if that had not happened, he would have had a chance to drive Abramovich's car full-time, to be the new Schumacher. He just gave a huge shrug. And, indeed, who knows?

But you have to believe that Jose Mourinho had been the long-time favourite for the high-performance driving seat. It just took a little time for someone to tell him. And how could he have imagined that, by the start of 2005,

Chelsea's growing stature was such that three of England's most celebrated players, David Beckham, Steven Gerrard and Michael Owen, were expected to be wearing blue shirts by the summer of that year?

Frank and the fans could see nothing but glory. There was a lot to play for.

10

Around the world, as the participants moved swiftly by private jet and luxury yacht and shiny, polished mahogany speedboats, the machinations went on to replace Claudio Ranieri with Jose Mourinho. It was never a question of if, simply when. For Frank and the rest of the Chelsea team there were always concerns. Yet for Frank personally, the coaching of Ranieri and the arrival of Abramovich had done nothing but good. His profile was soaring. He was a highly respected first-team player for both Chelsea and England. It hadn't seemed long ago that he'd have been happy to be in the England squad, even on the bench. Now such thoughts were heresy.

The strategists at this point were Ranieri and Eriksson. They had to get the ingredients right. And, although Ranieri rotated his players at a dizzying rate, Frank was always in there. The Tinkerman's tinkering never helped cohesion but, whatever the game plan, Frank always played a significant part and he always retained the capacity to surprise.

Which is why there was much disappointment when he turned out for England for the friendly against Portugal on 18 February 2004. The 1–1 draw said a lot about the team, but there was also discussion about how Frank was being played.

Much was written and much more said by the fans, but Paul Hayward in the *Daily Telegraph* got it spot on the day after the game: 'At Chelsea, Lampard is a puncher of holes, galloping from box to box to provide the team's midfield drive. At Stamford Bridge you will not find him in the team's Ryan Giggs position in front of the left back. He has neither the pace to get round the opposing right-back nor the natural inclination to distribute the ball with his left foot. It's not his fault.

'Lennox Lewis would give a horse a lousy ride in the Derby and Frankie Dettori would make a hopeless front-row forward. OK, so that is an exaggeration. It merely serves to illustrate the point that England will go into their opening match against France on 13 June with a deficiency Eriksson will somehow have to disguise.'

It was prescient about the competition in Portugal. It was also going to be quite a summer for Frank, Chelsea and England. Sven-Goran Eriksson is more sensitive than most in the football world and, some time before he announced the squad for Euro 2004, Frank knew that he would be playing a major role. There would be 'two teams' so that there was cover in every position, but Frank and Beckham and Steven Gerrard were pivotal. As was – fingers crossed – Wayne Rooney, the goal cannon.

The pundits kept saying that a style had to be developed to allow Frank to perform for England just as he did for Chelsea. What bigger praise? That the team had to accommodate his style – because he was a winner.

And Frank was on a run. Ranieri commented on his performance against Southampton on 1 May 2004, 'The outcome was decided in the space of eight minutes by goals from Frank Lampard – who else? I had read and heard about people saying that Frank's recent performances had not been as decisive as a few weeks before. These were foolish and inexpert comments. Frank Lampard had always been decisive for us, and besides, could anyone be so blind as to miss the point that I had been asking him for a big physical effort? Perhaps inordinately big, precisely because he was so fundamental to our cause.'

Claudio Ranieri was fired as manager of Chelsea on the May Bank Holiday weekend in 2004. His final game in charge was against Leeds at the Bridge on 15 May 2004, and for most of the second half the fans chanted his name. It was a victory for Chelsea, 1–0.

It was also a victory for Ranieri and his strength of character. As Ranieri's name echoed from the terraces, there was also a standing ovation for Frank and John Terry. Their outgoing manager paid tribute to them. 'They have been truly phenomenal this year but, best of all, they represent the real future of this team. A bright future, too, as there is nothing missing. The club has both money and the will to achieve.

'John Terry and Frank Lampard were already top players before working with me, as they had the right qualities within them. Perhaps I saw those qualities before they did and helped bring them out. I will always follow their progress and have a soft spot for them. They have become a part of me.'

Frank was with the England squad when Ranieri was sacked and he quickly got in touch with the former manager. He felt a strong bond with the man who had taken him over a bridge, from the traditions of West Ham to the glories of a continental Chelsea.

Understandably, it was a tense time for him. Here he was going into a major competition for his country, but what was happening to his role back at Chelsea? The commitment was all. Jose Mourinho pledged his allegiance. Sven-Goran Eriksson pledged his. All Frank Lampard had to do was play the game.

And for a very long time Frank Lampard was the star of England's debut in Euro 2004 at the Stadium of Light in Lisbon. It was hot in Portugal - and so was Frank. Towards the end of the first half of their opening game against France, David Beckham clipped over a ball to Frank. He headed it powerfully, beating Fabien Barthez: England 1 France 0.

Crucially, there was no encore. France came back with 88 minutes gone. The French captain, the captivating Zinedine Zidane, scored from a free-kick and a penalty. Stunned, Frank saw that glory eradicated, skilfully kicked away from under him.

For most of the match Frank had been England's greatest hero of the day. 'I have a very clear picture of that split second. It later sank in that, for a few minutes, I was a national hero. No one will even remember that I scored now.'

Of course, they do. And Jose Mourinho, Frank's unknown admirer, had been there to see the goal.

After the 2–1 defeat against France, England beat Switzerland 3–0, Croatia 4–2 and then met Portugal on their home turf. It's easier to draw a shroud over it but, to sum it up, it was the one where Wayne Rooney limped off and England said goodbye to Euro 2004, losing 6–5 on penalties.

For Frank it had been an incredible summer: one that for him showed nothing but promise. It was clear that he was the number-one man for England and Chelsea, a club that was now one of the most talked about in the world.

And at the same time another historical landmark was being established. Jose Mourinho, the engaging, brown-eyed, handsome 'special one' was the new boss. For Chelsea, football and Frank, it was a new world.

11

West Ham had held such a personal attachment for Frank that it had been difficult to say goodbye. Yet Chelsea had its own history. He made a point of learning how the club was formed in 1905 by the owners of the Stamford Bridge sports ground, and about how the current stadium (with a capacity of 42,449, though the record attendance is 82,905 for the First Division derby against Arsenal on 12 October 1935) forms part of Chelsea Village, a 12-acre leisure and entertainment complex in London SW6, which includes 291 four-star bedrooms, 21 conference and banqueting rooms, five themed restaurants and bars, and the Chelsea Club and Spa.

Frank went with Chelsea into their centenary year with ambitions of taking a unique haul of four trophies in one season: the Premier League, European Cup, FA Cup and Carling Cup. Not bad, especially when you consider their record. Their one League title to date had come in 1955, and there had been three FA Cup wins, two League Cups and two Cup-Winners' Cup wins. Chelsea now had the financial clout to go for it.

Abramovich bought Chelsea in July 2003 for £59.3 million. The Russian had already topped the *Sunday Times* 'Rich List' with a personal wealth of £7.5 billion, the highest in the UK. Which is why his football club was now creating some of the best training facilities in the world. They got the go-ahead to develop a £20 million training complex in Cobham, Surrey, to include a moat, 15 pitches, three with undersoil heating, plus an indoor pitch covered by a dome, one of Europe's largest physiotherapy departments and a headquarters built partly underground.

Which, naturally, was where Jose Mourinho came in. Or rather, jumped out. When he was officially named as the man in charge at Chelsea, he announced, 'I'm not one who comes straight out of a bottle. I'm the special one.' And so he proved.

On his appointment, the new manager said he would not discuss individual players, but he did say, 'I love Lampard.' Frank was then the most improved footballer in the English game. Both men were in it to win, for the glory and the cups. They are fighters, competitors, people who come out of watching Russell Crowe in *Gladiator* and see it as a motivational movie. You take on all the competition – and you win. Mourinho had that to do from the off.

He had to dismantle the past. When he was publicly named as the new boss at Chelsea on 2 June 2004, he immediately launched into Claudio Ranieri. Naughtily, Ranieri had recently suggested it was a lot easier to win the championship in Portugal than it was in England.

Mourinho said, 'Mr Ranieri says it's easy to win in Portugal and I didn't like what I heard. I could say other things like, "He is in football for 20 years and the only thing he won in his career is the Spanish Cup." I could say that. I don't like to, but I could.'

Ranieri was clearly upset about what had gone on and he took it out on the man closest to him – the man taking his job. He mocked Mourinho's claim that he would win trophies in his first season; he boasted about meeting Spurs earlier that week but, of course, he had turned down the manager's job at White Hart Lane for Valencia. At the same time he was working out a financial 'package' with Chelsea.

The clever Mourinho took every opportunity to establish himself and he had the advantage of having won the Champions League with Porto only a week earlier, and now of a three-year contract at Chelsea worth £4.5 million a season. He was obviously indignant at Ranieri's suggestion that he could only win in Portugal. 'You should explain to him that if a team wins the UEFA Cup or the Champions League, they have to play clubs from other countries.'

Mourinho, Peter Kenyon and Roman Abramovich flew by the owner's private jet to Manchester where they met Chelsea's four England players – Frank, Wayne Bridge, John Terry and Joe Cole – at the national squad's hotel on the eve of Euro 2004. For Frank it was another endorsement of how much he mattered to the team, and to the team's future.

The first he knew of the meeting was a telephone call in which he was simply told, 'He wants to see you.' They met for the first time in a private room at the hotel. Frank says his new boss stood in front of him, stared into his eyes and asked, 'Are you a winner?' 'It was a strange scene, but it felt right and walking out we all thought, we're going to win something this season.'

The late Sir Bobby Robson, who had made Mourinho his assistant at Barcelona, said, 'No one knows Jose better than me. He was my interpreter at Sporting Lisbon and stayed with me every day for six years. I see some players leave their careers and get a manager's job in a week. He didn't do that. He then spent two years with Louis van Gaal at Barcelona, so in total he spent eight years with two quite decent managers. We had a very good working relationship and, once he'd found his feet, he was on the pitch with me every day. He was a good student and a great help to me, but I think he learned a lot too. He was always very clever. He listened. He learned, he wrote down and remembered.

'He quickly realised the importance of establishing a rapport with the players. He had never been a player at a high level, so he respected what they could do. Jose was a great guy with the players and they appreciated that. I gave him more and more responsibility as time went on and we developed a mutual respect. He is now a top-class coach.'

But the best in the world? Better than Arsène Wenger or Sir Alex Ferguson? Jose Mourinho believed it. And Frank Lampard had no doubts.

12

As Frank continually pointed out, there was the manager's public face in the press conferences and the post-match television interviews, but with his players he was a different man. He was always a supporter. And he had total focus. In early 2005 he explained that one of the reasons he joined Chelsea was to help the club grow on and off the field. 'Peter Kenyon is completely focused on the Chelsea brand and making it one of the best clubs in the world. That makes me want to be part of the project.

'I always feel that with a president, or an owner, the players like to see him. When he comes here he is not coming to interfere with my work. He just comes to give us his faith, to give his support, to communicate with people. He's always present. He's committed. He knows what Mr Kenyon is doing, he knows what I am doing and he doesn't need to be worried about training players or the club organisation. Abramovich is a top man.

'I know how it works, though. I know football very well. I was nine or ten years old and my father was sacked on Christmas Day. He was a manager. The results had not been good. He lost a game on 23 December.

'On Christmas Day the telephone rang and he was sacked in the middle of our lunch. So I know all about the ups and downs of football. I know that one day I will be sacked. I know that one day the results will not be good...'

Time enough for that though. Back then the new manager made his mark on the world transfer market when, in July 2004, he made Didier Drogba the most expensive forward in the history of British football, paying £23.2 million for the Marseilles goal-maker. A further £8 million was invested in the Benfica midfielder Tiago taking the club's shopping bill to £31.2 million, a record single-day spend for a Premiership club.

They were soon joined by Petr Cech and the tremendous skills of Arjen Robben, Paulo Ferreira and Mateja Kezman, i.e. close on £70 million. The total cost of Chelsea's six close-season arrivals equalled that spent on new recruits by the rest of the Premiership put together.

Drogba echoed the new era at Chelsea when he said, 'I wanted to stay at Marseilles because I have experienced fantastic times there but financially, and in a sporting sense, I could not refuse Chelsea's offer.'

Mourinho was out to create a bunch of players who would conquer all. 'The big question mark,' he said, 'is how long will it take to impose my ideas on the team? I'll never forget Mario Stanic. He left the club but he was with me on the first day and said something like, "A lot of people have arrived in England and they adapt to the English reality of football. But I know that your methods and your philosophy and your way of thinking are very special. Don't ever change, even if it takes time, don't change." I'll never forget what he said.'

Long before Jose Mourinho achieved success as a coach, he thought of being a great player like his father, Felix Mourinho, who had kept goal for Vitoria Setubal, Belenenses and Portugal. As his only son, Jose was brought up to believe that he, too, had footballing genius within him.

But although Jose – 'Ze' to his team-mates – had great motivational ability, he was not a great defender. At 19 he could not command a first-team place with Rio Ave, the unfashionable First Division side that Felix was managing. A yellowing newspaper report of what happened then recounts, 'In 1982 came his chance. While warming up against Sporting Lisbon, Rio Ave's first-choice goalkeeper was injured and Felix summoned his son to the dressing room to get changed.

'Embarrassingly, he never made it on to the pitch. When Rio Ave's then president, Jose Maria Pinho, learned that Ze was about to wear Ave's green-and-white striped jersey, he issued an ultimatum: either Felix changes his decision or both he and his son are fired.

'Mourinho had to watch the match from the stands, where he saw his father's team lose 7–1.'

That was the point, it is said, when Mourinho decided that he would never be humiliated again and set his sights on becoming a top coach, even going so far as to expunge 'professional footballer' from his CV. The story also explains his methodical, unemotional approach to dealing with players and the almost perverse pleasure he seems to take in confronting management.

But, as the world looked on, it seemed as though there was nothing but big, blue skies for Jose Mourinho in August 2004. Chelsea wanted to win the Premiership. It was time to be number one.

13

'It was up to me to convince my players that Alex
Ferguson's problem was that he was scared of us.' That
is Jose Mourinho recalling a time when he was with Porto
and his club were up against Manchester United in the
Champions League. He explained further, 'At the time he
was a top manager... [he] felt he could beat us.'

He couldn't. And the rivalry, friendly but edgy, continued
in England when Chelsea leapfrogged up the table. Yet the
English Premiership of 2004-05 was very different from the
Champions League. Even before Christmas 2004, Mourinho
said, 'We have attitude and it will be difficult to catch us.'

The United manager and his players were very aware of
that but, as George Best pointed out in February 2005,
when you have to rely on another team to lose, the game is
usually already up.

Frank and the team were superbly pumped up for the 15
August 2004 game against United, their first major
encounter and test for the new boss. Before every match a
player is chosen by Mourinho to make a motivational
speech. Frank explained, 'It's about bonding and it's a way
of bringing out people's characters. We stand in the
dressing room, put our arms around each other and one of
us says a few words and finishes by asking, "Who are
we?!" Everyone shouts, "We are CHELSEA!!!"'

'There are a few lads, like Damien Duff, who are a bit

quiet and it's a way of bringing them out of themselves as well as getting everyone motivated. Scott Parker did the best one at Newcastle. It was the most aggressive speech I'd ever heard – about being ready for battle.

'The manager will have a joke, but the only thing that matters is winning. There is never a moment when you are allowed to relax. There's nothing that happens in a game that we haven't spoken about. He tells us we'll start in a particular way, but that if the game pans out differently then we will change and play this way. Everything is explained in such detail that the minute he does make a change we can adjust. We are able to do it because he leaves absolutely nothing to chance; he even tells us how to play if we go a goal up or down.

'He knows every opponent inside out. Even their subs. He talks to us as a team, but also individually. No player likes to be blanked by the manager, because even if you're playing well you still wonder what he's thinking.

'Before there wasn't quite the belief that there is now.'

That conviction was evident in Mourinho's first game with Chelsea against the man who would become his nemesis, Sir Alex Ferguson. They played lots of mind games, with both seeking the psychological advantage. After Porto's 2–1 win over Manchester United in the Champions League match in Portugal, Ferguson accused Mourinho's players of being from Central Casting – actors and divers.

Mourinho, showing that he was equally capable of playing with an opponent's mind, and observed that the Scottish manager had been 'a bit emotional' and was clearly upset to see his side 'dominated by a club with only 10 per cent of his budget'.

Contradicting the reports at the time, Mourinho says Ferguson never refused to shake his hand at the end of the game and that, when Porto went through on away goals with a late equaliser in the second leg at Old Trafford, he came to the dressing room to congratulate him. 'He felt he could maybe put some pressure on us,' Mourinho has said of Ferguson's pre-match remarks. 'I understood it. I work my players and I work the press conference to try to put a good atmosphere around my team. We play, we win, finish, shake hands. That's it.'

Well, nearly. To many, the game against Manchester United at Stamford Bridge that August was really about who were going to be the new kings of the Premiership. Mourinho was questioned before the game and was wonderful. 'I hope we have many, many rounds because if you have many rounds it means Sir Alex still feels young and stays at Manchester United and it means that my work is going well and I stay here for many seasons.'

Later, he went on, 'I'm a European champion and I think I'm a special one. If I wanted an easy job, I would have stayed at Porto – beautiful blue chair, the Champions League trophy, God, and, after God, me.'

Mourinho walked the tightrope between confidence, arrogance and superego. But the belief was relentless. He was certain Chelsea could win the Premiership in his first season in charge. 'The Chelsea I'm building will be a mixture of what I like in my teams and what I think is possible.'

And the head-to-head against United? 'If we win, we are not champions and, if we lose, we are not out of the fight. It is just one match, no more important than any other.'

But that's not how everyone saw it, especially Frank and the team. Frank said that before the encounter the new manager had told them: 'Let's have some fun.' And they certainly enjoyed themselves, despite the absence of Arjen Robben and Damien Duff. Chelsea scored an early goal through Eidur Gudjohnsen and then kept the lid on

United with the kind of display that so often proved beyond Claudio Ranieri's Chelsea sides.

'Mentally we were a team,' said a delighted Mourinho afterwards, but they were actually a good deal more than that. They were determined, disciplined and defensively strong, and what they lacked in invention they made up for in intelligence. Mourinho gave no championship guarantees, but he had made a good start: Chelsea 1 Manchester United 0.

Those in search of entertainment still found it, however. The contest that developed between Mourinho and the United fans provided anyone within earshot with an amusing alternative to the main event. Mourinho was surprised to discover opposing supporters in the seats immediately behind the dugouts at his new football home.

'In Portugal they are normally far away in a corner, behind a net,' said Mourinho. The proximity of rival fans meant he couldn't miss the invective which lurched between 'who the f**k are you?' to 'greasy foreigners'. Mourinho was cleverly polite. 'It was a beautiful song. Magnificent.'

One match report said, 'Mourinho sent out a Chelsea side with four new faces and no wingers and they performed in a way that made them look anything but strangers. We will see more from Drogba, who possessed pace and power but not enough poise, and the two he left on the bench, Mateja Kezman and Ricardo Carvalho. Of that there is little doubt.'

About Drogba and Carvalho it was right. The report went on, 'The self-proclaimed "special coach" tried to appear charitable in victory before asking the assembled media if he could be excused to join his wife on her birthday. "We deserved a victory but they didn't deserve a defeat," he said. "I said as much to Ferguson." Ferguson no doubt appreciated his new rival's generosity.'

The press loved seeing this young pretender tweaking the

nose of the old knight, Sir Alex Ferguson. And Mourinho revealed that the victory had been inspired by comments from Manchester United that a lack of team spirit at Stamford Bridge would cost them the title. On a day when champions Arsenal began with a comprehensive 4–1 win at Everton and were challenged by manager Arsène Wenger to go through the season unbeaten again, Mourinho took on United. 'What we showed today was that we have a great spirit because this was a performance which proved it.

'I told my players that they have to be ready to fight for each other in every moment of a match because they will not ever dominate for 90 minutes and that is what we did today.'

That summer Mourinho had made seven high-profile signings. This was the line-up of those bought and the media judgements on them:

RICARDO CARVALHO (£19.85m, Porto) His cool temperament and ability to second-guess the nippiest of forwards during Euro 2004 earned him the tag 'the new Beckenbauer' by a delighted Portuguese press. Should certainly be an improvement on the departed Marcel Desailly.

PAULO FERREIRA (£13.2m, Porto) Another import from Mourinho's former club, and another European Cup winner, but an unsteady showing at Euro 2004, particularly in the defeat by Greece in the opening game of the tournament, prompted a few questions about the size of his fee.

MATEJA KEZMAN (£5m, PSV Eindhoven) Last season's influx of strikers failed to make any lasting impression at Stamford Bridge. Serbia and Montenegro striker Kezman could buck that trend, but his biggest battle at the start of the season will be to earn and keep a starting place in Mourinho's team.

ARJEN ROBBEN (£12m, PSV Eindhoven) Another player to put in mixed performances at Euro 2004, Holland's zippy winger was slowed somewhat in Portugal by a nagging hamstring injury. The fully fit version should make a bigger impression in the Premiership.

TIAGO MENDES (£8m, Benfica) The third of the Portuguese imports, a midfielder with a big reputation back home, hence the £8 million fee. Like Kezman, will only really have the chance to shine if he gets a decent run in the starting line-up.

PETR CECH (£7m, Rennes) The Czech Republic's athletic goalkeeper will expect to oust Carlo Cudicini as Chelsea's No. 1. Whoever dons the gloves, though, Chelsea are guaranteed excellent cover from the bench, something they have lacked in previous years.

DIDIER DROGBA (£24m, Marseilles) Had a superb season with Marseilles, but one season doesn't make a superstar. An undoubted talent, Drogba is an immensely strong forward and is powerful in the air, but the size of that price tag brings with it a weight of expectation that could be his toughest opponent this season. The Ivory Coast man won the Player of the Year award in France last season and scored five goals in the Champions League followed by four in the UEFA Cup as Marseilles reached the final. The most expensive striker in the Premiership has linked well with Eidur Gudjohnsen in Chelsea's pre-season matches. Now for the real thing.

And what did Frank say? 'The manager was clever because he didn't bring in superstars who had done it all and had nothing to prove. He brought in brilliant players, admittedly very young and very hungry, who want to work for the

That's my boy! His uncle was the manager and his father was a West Ham coach but Frank's talent made a mockery of the nepotism chants.

Teenaged Rio Ferdinand came to tea at the Lampards – and signed on for West Ham where he and Frank became great mates. Rio's departure was the catalyst for Frank's move to Chelsea.

Above: How sweet it is – Frank celebrates another spectacular goal for Chelsea.

Below: Frank emerged in 2005 as the post-match spokesman for the team; his thoughts always calm, collected and quietly presented.

Jose Mourinho knew the way for Frank Lampard – the manager and his prized player celebrate another victory after their outstanding season together.

Above: Michael Owen salutes Frank's vital goal for England against France.

Below: A multi-million-pound line up: Wayne Rooney watches Frank and Rio Ferdinand enjoy another victorious England moment.

Above: On the ball: which foot will it be? He scores with them both and the fans are happy either way …

Below: Frank fan Sven-Goran Eriksson presents his regular player with the FA's England Player of the Year Award.

Above: A dejected Frank as England are knocked out of the 2006 World Cup by Portugal at the quarter finals.

Below: Warming up with Steven Gerrard during training ahead of a Euro 2008 qualifier against Israel.

Above and below left: Frank in action during Chelsea's FA Cup win over Everton in 2009.

Below right: Celebrating scoring the first goal against Croatia in the England World Cup qualifier at Wembley.

team. We haven't got a single individual who wants to be the main superstar. That's the club's strength.'

That and the lack of any fear whatsoever. Not many days after the defeat of Manchester United, Chelsea met Southampton at Stamford Bridge. The Blues had played four games and won four, Chelsea's best ever start to a season. The odds had dropped on the club bringing home the championship for the first time since Ted Drake's side in 1955.

Chelsea's next two matches were against Aston Villa away and Tottenham at home (both, as it turned out, goalless draws but, so importantly, not defeats) but Southampton was a hurdle.

Chelsea looked good as winners, once they took the lead. But there was much comment about how they would cope with being behind. They showed it against Southampton. James Beattie scored after just 12 seconds, the fourth-fastest goal in Premiership history, but Chelsea's response was positive even after that slam-bang impact stunned the capacity crowd. Gudjohnsen might have equalised after four minutes, when he headed Frank's inviting left-wing cross wide from six yards, then Drogba's left-footed shot was spilled by Antti Niemi, and Lampard, busily influential as ever, nearly tucked it away.

When the roles were reversed, Frank fired over from 20 yards after Drogba's strong incisive run, then was thwarted by the first of two goal-line clearances by Anders Svensson. It was all Chelsea, and the inevitable equaliser, after 34 minutes came as no surprise. A corner from Frank, bleeding from a cut around the eyebrow, was flicked on by Gudjohnsen, and Beattie turned the ball past his own goalkeeper.

Chelsea's superiority was such that the only question was how many more they would score. Tiago would have doubled the margin with a header, but for Svensson's second intervention under his own crossbar. The Saints' reprieve only lasted until 41 minutes when Claus Lundekvam, challenging Drogba in the air, handled the ball.

Frank scored the penalty and was named Man of the Match. Everything, it seemed, was going according to plan. Everything, it appeared, was sweet.

The always enthusiastic Gary Lineker had his take on Frank and Chelsea's future with Jose Mourinho. 'I have been hugely impressed by the way Mourinho has quickly created a team spirit. It's noticeable how he speaks regularly of the British and Irish players in his side, which may be a clever diplomatic ploy on his part, but I prefer to think it's because they are so essential to the team's success. You could argue that Frank Lampard, John Terry and Damien Duff are their spine.'

Or you might say the men with lots of backbone.

14

The summer of 2004 brought new awakenings – publicly at least – for Frank. Professionally, he was seen as Chelsea and England's ace in the hole. His work ethic had been superb.

'Someone at the Professional Footballers' Association should have a word with Frank Lampard. If they can get him to stand still long enough. While professional footballers cramp and creak under the workload of too many fixtures, Lampard is about to set a record for consecutive appearances by an outfield player. He is making his fellow athletes look like fair-weather joggers.'

That was Clive Tyldesley writing in the *Daily Telegraph* on 18 September 2004, who cleverly went on to point out, 'Three years ago he ran on at Stamford Bridge as a 73-minute substitute for Jimmy Floyd Hasselbaink against Leicester. Like Forrest Gump, Frank just kept on running.

'Three weeks ago, Lampard had to leave the field against Southampton to have a head wound stitched. Global warming would not normally be enough to make Jose Mourinho lose his cool, but the Chelsea manager was snarling and glowering like Sir Alex at his angriest when Lampard's absence stretched to several minutes.

'His orchestra had suddenly gone flat without the conductor. The heart of his team were missing a beat while their pacemaker was in for repair. Lampard will be the first name on his team sheet tomorrow. Even Claudio Ranieri knew not to tinker with Frank. The Chelsea squad rotate around their No. 8.

'Lampard's idea of a rest is playing for England at the European Championships. Since the start of last season he has clocked up 79 games for club and country.

'Last December, he was actually substituted in a couple of Premiership games. That was his winter break. But here's the rub. The most prolific feature of the record run is the relentless improvement in Lampard's performance level. The more he plays the more he grows in stature and influence. He is making a myth of the hard labour of modern football. Lampard's record-breaking fun run is a reminder that football isn't necessarily bad for your health.'

But history can be. For someone's emotional well-being anyway. In the weeks before Tyldesley's glowing endorsement of his marathon-man dedication, details had surfaced of the Lampard family past.

It had been a difficult time for Frank and his family. And a quiet, private time. All involved are reluctant to discuss or go into pertinent details of the full background. There are indications that much of the story had been known in the East End for many years but, because of the admiration for Frank Senior, it was simply acknowledged rather than admitted. One family friend who approached Frank Senior about it found that what had been seen as a strong, loving relationship was, in reality, not quite the case.

On 4 July 2004, it was made public that Frank had a half-sister, Sophie, born a year after him, and a half-brother, John, born towards the end of his father's playing career. Sophie and John Butler were born when Frank Lampard Senior was a West Ham star.

Their mother, Janet, was the other woman in his life for clearly some years. When he was approached about the situation in July 2004 by the *News of the World* he said, 'I accept what I did was wrong. This was an episode in my life that was some time ago and it is important that I draw a line under it now.'

The difficult revelations posed many questions. Did Harry Redknapp know about Janet Butler? Did Frank Senior's drinking mates at the Black Lion? 'In those days you kept some things under your hat. There was lots of stuff best left in the dressing room,' said the journalist Jeff Powell.

It was suggested to me that Pat Lampard knew about 'the other family', but that she lived with that knowledge in the interests of her own family's harmony. This was never confirmed or denied to me, despite many enquiries.

What is known is that Sophie and John – Frank's half-siblings – live with their mother not that far away from their father's family home in Romford. Sophie, it was revealed, was conceived 10 weeks after Frank Senior did his baby pictures with Pat and new son Frank. John arrived nearly five years later. Frank Senior's name does not appear on either of his other children's birth certificates.

The *News of the World* quoted the family 'friend', who leaked the story to the paper, as saying that Sophie and John had been 'hidden away'. It said that they lived in 'a modest terraced home' in Ilford in east London. It was also reported that Frank Senior did see Sophie (he appeared on her re-registered birth certificate in 1995) and John 'now and again'.

All of which makes us wonder how much subterfuge was going on within the family. Who knew what? As of March 2005, Frank had said nothing about his 'new' brother and sister. His father added, 'I ask that I'm left alone with my family. I would like to thank the *News of the World* for dealing with this story so sensitively.'

The story of the Lampard 'secret family' had appeared at a difficult time. The Frank Lampards, father and son, were appearing in television advertisements for Sainsbury's supermarkets with Jamie Oliver, playing the happy family.

Whatever went on, it did not affect Frank on the pitch. He played as if his only concern in the world was scoring goals and winning.

And, despite the family turbulence, his life seemed to have settled. Gone were the gossip column stories that he'd 'bagged' Liz McLarnon from Atomic Kitten or had been in this or that nightclub. He'd moved to a sumptuous apartment in Knightsbridge, close to Stamford Bridge, and he had found a meaningful girlfriend in Elen Rives. Of his Spanish girlfriend he said, 'I'm happy and when you're happy in your life it makes everything easier. It's the first real relationship I've ever been in.

Elen, who was close to Steven Gerrard's partner Alex Curran and John Terry's girlfriend Toni Poole, also became involved with one of Frank's important interests outside of football. He is a fervent supporter of the Teenage Cancer Trust and regularly visits their unit at the Middlesex Hospital. 'I just sit around and chat. The time passes very quickly. I'm not certain what I do – I hope I'm helping them along. But what I do doesn't seem very much.'

What's telling is that he did not make one PR visit, but continues to do so and asks for contributions to be made in his name to the Teenage Cancer Trust (Teenage Cancer Trust, 38 Warren Street, London WIT 6AE) rather than accept most media fees. He has pledged himself as a lifelong supporter of the trust.

15

In early 2005 it looked as though Frank and Chelsea could achieve a string of sporting miracles. Could Chelsea win the FA Cup, Premiership, Carling Cup and European Cup in one season, which would have meant that the bookies faced a £20 million payout? When they were knocked out of the FA Cup by Newcastle 1–0 (with 10 men for much of the match and nine by the end), on a bitterly cold, snow-swept 20 February 2004, the bookies saved a fortune.

In fact the bookies had been slow to spot the Chelsea rollercoaster. Hills were offering 400-1 on the Big Four at the beginning of the season and most of the bets being made were by small-time punters with a £5 or £10 long shot. But, once the totting-up started, the bookies realised they had a potential disaster looming. By the middle of February 2005, they were quoting Chelsea as 9–2 favourites to win the European Cup, despite the fact that the experts expected Barcelona to trounce them over the two legs in the next round.

Big money and Chelsea went hand-in-hand. It was predicted that Chelsea would be one of the three richest clubs in Europe. The respected accountancy firm Deloitte reported in their Money League on 17 February 2005 that Chelsea, Manchester United and Arsenal would be the new Big Three, overshadowing Real Madrid and Barcelona.

The Money League covered the 2003-04 season. Manchester United were Europe's wealthiest club with earnings of £171.5 million, slightly down on the year before. Chelsea, boosted by Abramovich's wealth, were fourth, behind Real Madrid and AC Milan. But they earned £143.7 million which made them, with Barcelona, the fastest growers in the financial race. Chelsea jumped six places in the wealth league, despite having only a 42,449-seat stadium, and the report concluded, 'They will not think that future overall leadership is beyond them. With Chelsea's success and Arsenal's Emirates Stadium development, we can foresee a scenario where English clubs fill the top three places in the 2006-07 Money League.'

The report listed Britain's Top 10:

REVENUE SOURCES (IN MILLIONS)

	Matchday	Broadcasting	Commercial	Average gate
Manchester Utd	61.2	62.5	47.8	67,500
Chelsea	53.6	56.4	33.7	39,700
Arsenal	33.8	59.8	21.4	36,600
Liverpool	26.4	33.5	32.4	41,800
Newcastle Utd	33.9	33.7	22.9	50,000
Celtic	34.7	16.1	18.2	56,000
Tottenham	19.8	23.9	22.6	34,100
Manchester City	17.1	25.5	19.3	43,800
Rangers	24.2	7.5	25.4	47,200
Aston Villa	12.4	27.2	16.3	35,600

**EUROPE'S TOP 20 RICHEST CLUBS
(POSITION FOR PREVIOUS YEAR IN BRACKETS)**

Total revenues for 2003-04 in £ million

1.	Manchester Utd (1)	171
2.	Real Madrid (4)	156.3
3.	AC Milan (3)	147.2
4.	Chelsea (10)	143.7
5.	Juventus (2)	142.4
6.	Arsenal (7)	115
7.	Barcelona (13)	112
8.	Inter Milan (6)	110.3
9.	Bayern Munich (5)	110.1
10.	Liverpool (8)	92.3
11.	Newcastle Utd (9)	90.5
12.	Roma (11)	72
13.	Celtic (18)	69
14.	Tottenham (16)	66.3
15.	Lazio (15)	65.8
16.	Manchester City (-)	61.9
17.	Schalke (14)	60.5
18.	Marseilles (-)	58.3
19.	Rangers (-)	57.1
20.	Aston Villa (-)	55.9

Chelsea's first accounts under Ambramovich's ownership had shown just how costly it is to create and maintain an A-plus squad of players. The accounts showed that the Russian had invested £100 million of equity into the business and provided a further £115 million in the form of an interest-free loan with no specific repayment date. That was in addition to the original £59.3 million the club cost Abramovich.

In the year to June 2004, Chelsea made an operating loss of £13.1 million. The cash outflow for that period was

£161.7 million – and not even Abramovich could sustain that consumption of cash forever.

Just over £175.1 million went in buying players from 2003–4. Another £115.5 million was paid out in wages – Frank being one of the highest-paid players – bonuses and other remuneration. And about 35 members of the Chelsea business earned £2 million, making the club more generous than the world's biggest and most successful investment banks. But it would need sustained success on the pitch if Chelsea Football Club were to become a cash-generative, self-sustaining business.

For all the money involved, Frank's game was not just football but helping the team bond together. The Serbian Mateja Kezman, bought by Chelsea from PSV Eindhoven in the summer of 2004 for £5 million, wasn't doing that well. He'd scored just one goal, against West Ham in the Carling Cup. Soon after he came on as a substitute in the Chelsea v Newcastle Premiership game and hit the post. 'I almost cried when that didn't go in,' recalled Chelsea's assistant manager Steve Clarke. But in the last moments of the game Chelsea won a penalty. Frank, the normal penalty taker, handed the ball to Kezman knowing what it would mean to him to score his first Premiership goal. Kezman delivered.

In that moment all the work that Mourinho had been doing, the bonding, the 'Are you a winner?' mantra came good. 'When we were given the penalty I went to Frank and asked him if I could take it,' remembered Kezman, adding, 'he gave me the ball because he knows how difficult it had been for me with no goals. Goals are my life. When you score 20 or 30 goals every year for the past seven or eight years and then just one in three months it's very hard.

'You could see our spirit after I scored. Every single player came to me. That was fantastic. That was our strength that season. That's how we knew we could be champions. Frank Lampard did that for me...' And for the team, which won 4–0.

Oliver Holt of the *Mirror* said in his match report, 'You can't buy Frank Lampard handing the ball to Kezman in those dying seconds. You can't buy the sight of every tired player in the Chelsea side engulfing Kezman in his happiness. You can't buy the gratitude he felt to his team-mates or the confidence such an audacious penalty will bring. Lampard's brilliance is becoming almost monotonous. He is producing match-winning performances week after week after week. He has become the complete player.'

But Frank had already been cast in that role in the run-up to the race for the Premiership. A glance back to Halloween in 2004, when Chelsea played West Bromwich Albion at the Hawthorns, shows that. It was all about character. They had suffered the 'nightclub' reporting of footballers' excesses (Adrian Mutu of Chelsea had been fired for taking cocaine and there had been lurid headlines about footballers gambling in casinos), but on the day won 4–1.

Chelsea's third goal owed a lot to Lampard. He carried the ball 40 yards before picking out Duff with an exquisite pass, who cut in and scored from 12 yards. Then, latching on to a pass from Arjen Robben, Lampard applied the fourth from 20 yards. He was taken off by Mourinho to an ovation from the Chelsea faithful.

16

Frank Lampard was acknowledged as one of England and Chelsea's greatest players in 2005. You can't, of course, put it all down to hard work, to that extra training, the parental encouragement and work ethic. There's the 'it' factor, the talent, the magic. As Claudio Ranieri said, 'If the marble is good I can improve the player.'

In Frank's case it seemed more solid gold than marble, considering his incredible improvement and rise to distinction in international football. A year earlier he was no more than a cameo player for Sven-Goran Eriksson, now he was one of the star turns. And now even more so for Jose Mourinho.

With their new leader, Frank believed there were few limits to his and Chelsea's future. Frank pointed out, 'In training, everything is now done with a ball. Before, a lot of it was physical stuff with the fitness coach. Under Mourinho, virtually everything we do is intended to replicate a match situation. That has helped the players technically and made us more tactically aware.

'The work we do with a ball, day in day out, is the foundation of the team's strength. We look strong and solid because we hammer away at getting it right every day in training. The organisation is becoming ingrained.

'It's not that we've just got the one way of playing, but if we do change we really do know what we're doing because it has been mapped out beforehand. In the build-up to the game the manager will have prepared us for every possibility. He'll say, "If this happens, we might change to this."

'It's never off-the-cuff, as it was under Ranieri, it's always something that has been pre-planned. The manager knows how productive free-kicks and corners can be. If you get it right, the delivery, the routine and the movement, you'll score goals.

'In my case, I'm taking free-kicks and corners, which I was never entrusted with before. He has given me that responsibility, it's something I've added to my game and it has made me believe in myself even more. He is bringing out the best in me. What I haven't got is as many goals and that's something that bothers me, because I think like a striker – if I haven't scored I'm not happy no matter how well I've played. I do need to be among the goals.

'We spend more time on that than we did under Claudio Ranieri, not just on the training pitch but in team meetings, after watching the opposition.

'There is a rule book. But because I came back late after the Euros I didn't get my copy until two weeks later. The papers made a lot about its contents – more than is actually in there. There are guidelines, governing punctuality and the like, but they are not as strictly applied as people have made them out to be.

'There is one main rule, which is that you behave like a professional at all times. Otherwise, if you are late for training or whatever, he will always listen to your reason. He doesn't crack down with an iron fist straight away.

'As regards socialising, it's not as the press reported it, that we must be in by midnight on such and such a day or 1am on another. What he is saying is, "As long as you're sensible, and go out at the right times, that's fine by me, but if you go out drinking the day before a match, or the night before training, you're not going to be able to train or play as I want you to."

'He's very approachable. I was comfortable with him right from the start, and I think all of us felt that way. He gave me confidence. We've gone from 4-4-2 to 4-3-3 and we keep the ball a lot more. There are times when we want to take the sting out of games, and now we can really do that.'

Mourinho had a clear idea from the start how he wanted Frank to fit into his Chelsea team. 'He can remain the same individually, but I want to change him in relation to the team, like we did with Deco at Porto. It all depends on what the team needs from him. If one day I tell Frank I don't want him to be a box-to-box player, but to hold back, he has to adapt to our needs.

'We put a stamp on a player and say "he's this type", but sometimes that player has to be different. He was used to playing side by side with Makelele, but I've got him playing a different line to Makelele.'

If there was a criticism of Mourinho's Chelsea, it was that they were not as exciting to watch as Manchester United or Arsenal. The truth was, like the Arsenal of old, they were happy to win 1–0. 'We all are,' said Frank. 'The manager does like to play good football; he's not one of those who wants to defend, content to play unattractive football and nick a result. He'd be happier, obviously, winning 3–0, but 1–0 will do as well.

'I've got the licence to get forward whenever I want to, as long as I can get back when needed as well. It's nice to have the insurance of "Maka" [Makelele] behind me. Because he's always there, I can push on.'

Frank now had the stature of an England player. 'Before the Euros, I'd played 20 times, but often as a substitute, and you don't feel comfortable until you're starting games.

It's only after you've had a run in the side that you start to feel that you belong. That feeling flowed through me in Portugal and now I view the England situation entirely differently. I'm part of the team and expect to be starting.'

And that had been the dream since his father first threw a ball at his feet.

On top of that, Chelsea now had a chance of winning four trophies. George Best, who lived a stone's throw from Stamford Bridge, focused on their hopes. One thing he was certain about was that his beloved Manchester United would not win the Premiership. 'Never mind the maths. When you've got to rely on others losing, you might as well turn it in. You can't go on hoping Chelsea might drop a point here or there. It doesn't work that way. Chelsea are running away with it. Rightly so, the way they play.'

Best was equally complimentary of Chelsea's flamboyant manager. 'Jose Mourinho is a breath of fresh air. Some people say he's a flash bastard, but you can only get away with that if you're really good. Sure, he's spent a lot, but a lot of managers spend big money. It's what you get with it that counts. Me, I love him. You see, he does the little things well. He gets his players to throw their shirts to the crowd. Or Scunthorpe turn up for a cup game and he makes them feel welcome. He puts on a show for them.

'Some of the great ones did that. Sir Matt [Busby], Shankly, Nicholson, Stein, Clough. They all tried to do the little things well. It's important. And he's got an awesome side. I mean, even when they're poor, the worst they get is a point. That's the way you win the title.'

The furore over the so-called approach by Chelsea to Arsenal's Ashley Cole hardly shocked Best. 'They say they're tapping people, is that right? Nothing new there. They tapped me once. It wasn't what you'd call subtle. They just told the press they'd like me in their team. No big deal.

They weren't the only ones. I had both the Milan clubs, Real Madrid, and one or two others. But they were all wasting their time. We were winning things, weren't we? I mean, we won the big one, the European Cup. You couldn't leave a team like that.

'Still, it was interesting the way they went about it. You'd see them in the players' lounge and they'd give you a card and say, "If you're ever in Madrid or Milan, perhaps we could have lunch?" Tricky people these foreigners. Chelsea were different. They just came right out with it.'

Best, like many others, admired Mourinho's man-management. Gordon Strachan, who as player-coach with Coventry famously and sympathetically put a comforting arm around Frank when the West Ham crowd welcomed him with that spiteful loud booing, said, 'You might not see managers as agony aunts but, oh dear, some of the things we've heard. Some of the kids come from tough homes. They have lots of problems.

'Footballers get the blame for yobbish behaviour but, if you think about it, they're yobs before they get here. If you've got a yob and he meets money, it's a hell of an explosive combination. To be a good coach, like Mourinho, is like being a good doctor. You take an oath to make people better. It's the manager's responsibility to teach young players respect... I always told every player of mine to come to me if they had a problem.'

Maybe he still had the festive spirit, but it was in early January 2005 that Mourinho played happy host to Scunthorpe (League Two) in the incident Best recalled. Chelsea did the job on the field (they won 3–1), but the manager won the good-grace stakes. The man who created a career out of influencing people was now winning friends, too. He gave the freedom of Stamford Bridge to opponents almost 70 places beneath him in the football pecking order.

When Scunthorpe arrived on Saturday morning to familiarise themselves with the stadium, Mourinho acted as their tour guide. Before they left, he presented them with his scouting report that had contributed to their downfall. Scunthorpe manager Brian Laws said, 'Mourinho treated us like kings and we nearly took a ransom. When we shook hands at the end he said, "With that luck we will win the championship."

'Maybe he can be a bit arrogant and bigheaded, but he has a personality like Brian Clough and I say that by way of a huge compliment because Brian was a legend. Jose made my players feel very special. People call him ruthless and rude, but that isn't the Jose Mourinho I met. He took us into their dressing room and told us to talk with everyone, get shirts and autographs. He made it one of the great days for all of us.'

John Hollins, a player, coach and manager at Chelsea in very different days to the ones he witnessed in 2004 and 2005, had firm belief in Mourinho's ability to lead Chelsea to glory. 'Winning all four trophies is on, of course it is. It requires consistency and Chelsea have proved they have that. The attitude must be right and they have that, too. It requires a marvellous team spirit and it's obvious in the way they play that they have that.

'You need class players and Chelsea have them in abundance. And, perhaps most importantly, it is essential that the team is run by a manager the players respect and who respects the players. Well, in Jose Mourinho, they certainly have such a man. And, if they survive Barcelona, everything is possible.'

Hollins led Chelsea into more battles than any player in the club's history during the sixties and seventies. But while they excelled in the cups – Hollins played in the famous FA

Cup Final replay victory over Leeds United in 1970 – a lack of consistency was their downfall.

While the contrast between the resources available to the two men as managers was astonishing, Hollins could see similarities between the Mourinho era and his own playing days. 'We were a team in the real sense. We had the right attitude and so do Mourinho's team. The first Chelsea team I played in as a 17-year-old, the 1964 side, had Terry Venables, Eddie McCreadie, Barry Bridges and George Graham. We were young and confident and could outrun anyone else in the First Division. Isn't that an outstanding quality of the present team, too: to run and work for each other, to want to play – no, to *desire* to play for Chelsea?

'Yes, he has the money he needs to buy the very best. I remember how difficult things were when I was manager. Once I couldn't believe how long the grass was getting. I asked why it hadn't been cut and was told they owed money on the mower and weren't allowed to use it. I gave the groundsman £50 of my own money and told him to go out and buy anything that would solve the problem.

'But it's not only the money. Mourinho also has scientific knowledge that was not available to us. For example, as players we used to have a big steak and rice pudding before every match. We now know it takes five hours to digest that sort of meal, but we weren't aware of that then, yet in a couple of hours we'd be out there running like hares.

'It helps when you know. Jean Tigana, for example, when he was coach at Fulham, used to insist on regular hands, feet and teeth examinations. You can discover a lot from the condition of teeth. If we had a toothache we'd just ask for a tot of whisky, but it wouldn't stop us playing.

'Now if you have so much as a sniffle you are left out –

although I noticed John Terry, who has been outstanding, coughing hard in the warm-up before the Middlesbrough game. I thought then that he was taking a big chance if he had failed to tell them he wasn't 100 per cent.'

As the title race intensified, the debate went on and on about Chelsea, the world's most talked-about team. The ongoing question: could money buy success? Fans of all persuasions were having their say. Edie May-Bedell, a Leeds fan who had seen his club bankrupt itself in the pursuit of glory, wrote, 'I support Leeds, so I know the trauma of what can happen when a team tries to buy its way to the top. However, I am fed up of the anti-Chelsea bias in the media. So they have lots of money. What do you think Manchester United and Arsenal have spent – a shiny sixpence and half a crown? It seems ludicrous to set a limit on what is an acceptable amount of obscene wealth. Are millions good and super-millions bad?

'We should welcome a team that can at last break the dominance of United and Arsenal. The implied criticism that Chelsea are only top because of Roman Abramovich's millions is both wrong and insulting to the hard work done by Jose Mourinho and his team. Do they have too much money? Yes, but so do all top teams.'

Chelsea member Matthew White added, 'For years we have been disliked (hated would be so overdramatic) for the sole reason of a thorough disliking for Ken Bates. To an extent I can understand this. None of this really mattered because for 26 years Chelsea never won anything and never seriously challenged for the League title.

'Now things have changed and suddenly we are becoming everybody's punch bag. Yes, we have spent money, but so have Man Utd and others for years. I don't remember cries of Liverpool being bad for the game when, already the No.1 side in the country in the 1980s, they went out and bought John Barnes and Peter Beardsley, two of the most sought-after properties of the time.

'Is the introduction of Robben, Cech, Makelele and Drogba bad for the game? Above all, is Mourinho bad for the game? Surely he is the best thing that has happened to the Premiership this season. Forget about Fergie and Wenger's handbags, Mourinho is the man and blue is the colour.'

Sol Campbell of Arsenal, understandably, disagreed. 'In my time at Arsenal I've noticed anyway that we don't really kick on until the last 10 or 15 games. Some players, some teams, run out of steam. You've got someone (Roman Abramovich) who doesn't care about money, so of course you can get players from all over the world. Then you've got a new manager coming in. Everyone wants to work hard. It's normal. But no one can keep up that kind of tempo all season. It's impossible.'

Not so partisan was David Platt, who won the UEFA Cup with Juventus, and believed England's best chance of winning the Champions League in 2005 was with Chelsea. 'Mourinho has proved he knows what it takes. The most attacking teams generally find it hard to win the Champions League. If it means playing a bit more negatively, Mourinho will say fine. He will do anything, change anything, to win.'

After Chelsea beat Newcastle 4–0 in December 2004, Newcastle manager Graeme Souness said, 'They are a team filled with top players and they are the team to catch now. But you'd be a fool to say nobody can catch them. I don't think people in Manchester or north London think the game is up yet.'

And in the same month, Alex Ferguson was calling Frank Lampard's constant performances 'freakish' and clearly regarded Chelsea as the biggest threat to his team. After using his mind games to undermine Arsenal in previous weeks, the United boss turned his attentions to Mourinho's Premiership leaders by questioning whether the Londoners had the stamina to stay the course, as they looked to become champions for the first time in half a century.

'Chelsea will go close in both the Premiership and the Champions League,' said Ferguson, 'but the thing is that so far the only thing they have done is go close. Jose Mourinho has done well so far. He has got Chelsea in a position where everybody is now wondering how they are going to be caught.

'It will be a hard task to catch them, but the key thing is that as a team they have no experience of winning the games that really, really matter, like we have and like Arsenal have. Chelsea will get a blip – I have no doubt that they will lose a game or two.

'And there have been a lot of clubs before Chelsea who have looked in control all season, only to see the title fly out of the window in March. Both ourselves and Arsenal have been through the mill for a number of years now and that's the advantage we have over Chelsea.

'Mourinho has surprised me by picking strong teams for the League Cup. Maybe it was to be expected in the quarter-final because it was a local derby against Fulham, but I have heard that they are now talking about winning all four competitions. I don't know about that. My maxim is that it is a good achievement to win one trophy every year and anything else is a bit greedy.'

Chelsea were definitely that, as both the weeks and games ticked on...

17

Frank Lampard had plenty of fire in his belly and a great incentive to win honours with Chelsea. So far he had only a 2002 FA Cup loser's medal (losing 2–0 to Arsenal on 5 May 2002) and an InterToto Cup winners medal. For that other Upton Park graduate Joe Cole, the only proof of his remarkable skill was winning the FA Youth Cup with West Ham.

But they and their team-mates were now producing breathtaking football, with a settled shape and a strong defence, choreographed by Jose Mourinho. Chelsea's spirit was outstanding and Frank and John Terry were strong contenders for Footballer of the Year.

The oddball was the manager. Jose Mourinho was in charge of arguably the biggest and strongest football club in the world and, at times, one wondered if he believed that his personality should match that. Only the gloom merchants were dismayed by Mourinho's swagger. Thousands wanted the new force to unsettle the dominance of Arsenal and Manchester United. They loved the bright new spark but in the key, last week of February 2005, Mourinho seemed overcharged.

At times it was embarrassing. The manager who had ridden into town like Clint Eastwood, with the stubble if not the cheroot, suddenly found himself looking lost. And losing crucial football games.

Sir Alex Ferguson's prediction was right. The Chelsea 'blip' did happen. Against Newcastle United in the FA Cup Mourinho made a dramatic triple substitution at half-time but then lost Wayne Bridge to a foot injury and his 10 remaining men lost the match.

From the cold and despondency of Newcastle, Frank and the others flew off to Spain for their confrontation with Barcelona with the critics snapping at their heels. From the coverage you'd think they'd lost their lives not a game against Newcastle. Frank said, 'Everyone has been waiting for it to happen, to make a big deal out of it. It comes with the territory of being a team which wins a lot. I think Arsenal probably got it when they finally lost a game.'

Yet there were more problems in Barcelona. The sending-off of Didier Drogba at the Nou Camp was a controversial moment which changed the face of a game that Chelsea had got back into but then lost 2–1. To all the commentators this was blip number two. According to some reports, the Chelsea squad and their leader were cracking up.

But then the focus shifted to the manager again. Mourinho, dragging the focus away from his team's performances, put himself into the spotlight. He complained that Frank Rijkaard, the much-liked and respected Barcelona coach, had talked with the referee at half-time (something of a Mourinho obsession) and also that he'd been kicked in the backside (later denied) by one of Rijkaard's assistants in a tunnel incident. He then refused to attend the post-match press conference.

It was like his run-in with Sir Alex Ferguson in January 2005, whom he accused of influencing the match referee at half-time in the Carling Cup semi-final. 'I believe he was just playing games,' said BBC pundit Gary Lineker, adding, 'I am fairly sure he was just trying to sneak what tiny advantage could.' Or maybe he was diverting attention from the score. Yet he had made a series of mistakes, starting with the three-man substitution against Newcastle.

Mourinho retaliated, saying, 'We are not a club with a culture of winning like Manchester United, Juventus, Milan and Real Madrid, clubs who have had years to construct a team. If you want to have a short memory or put pressure on Chelsea, just mention the amount of money spent over the last two years and demand more victories. But there is no reason to be unhappy. They can't talk about blips.'

For Frank it was an unsettling week, but one which he had mentally prepared for. He is so steeped in football and in the history of the game that he knows it's not just a beautiful one but also a cruel one.

The Newcastle defeat was a shock, Barcelona a hurdle. Diplomatically, Frank's then girlfriend Elen Rives, a Catalan, never revealed which team she was cheering for. More importantly for Frank and Chelsea was whether they, as a side, used to the constant knockabout of Premiership football, could deal with future European pressure where wins develop more often through science than chance, and where possession of the ball is a way of life, not a momentary thing.

After Newcastle and Barcelona their war games continued against Liverpool in a head-on, one-off clash for the Carling Cup. It was Frank's big chance for a solid silver trophy. And Chelsea were the favourites.

At the Millennium Stadium in Cardiff, Roman Abramovich nervously watched his players take on a determined Liverpool after their shaky week in Newcastle and Barcelona. And it was a nail-biting beginning for Chelsea fans. After only 45 seconds Fernando Morientes skilfully moved the ball to the far post and John Arne Riise put a powerful volley into the Chelsea net. And for nearly 80 minutes, what looked like an eternity for Abramovich in the stand and Mourinho on the line, Liverpool remained one goal up.

For much of the game Chelsea had possession but were blocked by Liverpool's defence. The frustrated Mourinho kept shouting at his squad, 'Come on. Come on!'

He took off Gallas and substituted Kezman, the score-starved import Frank had helped get his first Premiership goal, and the game changed. Suddenly. Frank swooped through the middle of the field and over the halfway line when he was brought down. Paulo Ferreira belted in the free-kick, which Liverpool's captain Gerrard helped into the net for an own goal. It brought an obvious response following all the transfer talk about Gerrard and Chelsea. Was this his first goal for the Blues?

The equaliser set off a Chelsea clamour, and Mourinho turned to the Liverpool fans who had been taunting him and put his finger to his lips, signalling 'Hush'. Later, he said it was to silence the British press, but the crowd safety officer decided that the Chelsea manager had to go – banished to the television company's control room. That's where he watched the rest of the game. The only commentary was him shouting at the television set.

Extra time brought out the best in Chelsea and tiredness in Liverpool. Even Liverpool's anthem 'You'll Never Walk Alone' couldn't get the Kop squad's legs working full-time. You could see them slowing down.

Frank clapped his hands time and time again, cheering on his team-mates. Up in the stands Abramovich had his head in his hands at times. Mourinho? Presumably he was still shouting at the silent television.

In what seemed like a moment, we were in the second half of extra-time. Glen Johnson, that other Upton Park graduate, had come on for Joe Cole, and it was his throw-in which allowed Drogba the chance to score from close range in the 107th minute.

Five minutes later and Frank was in the thick of the action. His free-kick was hammered against Dudek by Gudjohnsen and, in the moments of muddle, the fresh-legged Kezman was there to poach, to sneak Chelsea's third goal over the line. A minute later Antonio Nunez headed in Gerrard's free-kick, but it was too late for Liverpool.

Chelsea had won the Carling Cup.

In a pantomime sequence, Mourinho was escorted by a Football League lawyer from his banishment and wandered around the pitch congratulating and hugging his players. He shook hands with everyone – including Steven Gerrard. There was talk of fines and investigations, but for most people in Cardiff all that had mattered was the result. 'You cannot underestimate how important winning the Carling Cup was to Chelsea. If there was ever the case of the performance not mattering, this was it,' said commentator Alan Hansen after the game, adding, 'It was massive for Chelsea. They have come off the back of two defeats, they have lost a goal in the first minute of a Cup final and the manager goes on a walkabout among Liverpool supporters. If they had been beaten by Liverpool, even on penalties, it would have been catastrophic.

'If they had lost for the third time in a week it's conceivable they would have ended up with nothing. It's a funny thing pressure. It was starting to build up on Chelsea, but the result in Cardiff has washed away much of it. It makes a massive difference to them mentally.'

Mourinho had been shuffled off stage at the Millennium Stadium, while Frank and John Terry, with Joe Cole and the imported goal-seekers, put on a brilliant show. They kissed and held up the cup, soaked in sweat and champagne spray, the second leg with Barcelona now only days away. It was what Alex Ferguson calls 'squeaky bum time' with the Premiership now racing to a conclusion.

18

The evening of 8 March 2005 was a momentous one at Stamford Bridge. Just seven minutes into their second leg against Barcelona, Eidur Gudjohnsen scored Chelsea's first goal, bringing the aggregate score to 2–2. Nine minutes later, Frank added a second from close range, following up Joe Cole's cross.

Two minutes on, it was the softly spoken, amiably shy Damien Duff's turn, with Joe Cole's help, sweeping the ball through the legs of the advancing Barcelona keeper Victor Valdes for 3–0 on the night. All looked good and then suddenly it was a hands-over-the-eyes moments for the Chelsea fans as well as for Roman Abramovich.

The Spanish side retaliated with a penalty from Ronaldinho, wiping out Chelsea's away goal and bringing the aggregate score to 4–3 to Chelsea. One more goal for Barcelona would send them through, and 11 minutes later it came, the Brazilian star scoring with a clever 20-yarder.

But it was only half-time. On the terraces, the crowd could hardly watch as the drama became more intense. Frank had vowed after the so-called blip, 'We'll bounce back.' And that evening they did just that, with John Terry providing the 'boy's own' moment. The Chelsea skipper headed a precious winner from Damien Duff's out-swinging corner 14 minutes from time to make it 4–2 and 5–4 on aggregate.

The final whistle from referee Pierluigi Collina triggered chaotic scenes. The Barcelona manager Frank Rijkaard and his players took exception to a crowing response to victory by Jose Mourinho's scout, Andre Villas. Stewards had to intervene and Eto'o, who claimed he was called a monkey, allegedly spat at a steward. The row raged in the tunnel.

Barcelona fans then became involved, pelting Mourinho with plastic bottles for blowing kisses at them and launching missiles at Roman Abramovich. The Chelsea owner ignored them – he was intent on reaching the home dressing room.

Rijkaard tried to play down the tunnel incident and said, 'It was not a big deal. You know what it's like when emotions run high. Some guy, I have no idea who he was, came over at the final whistle and said something. He insulted our bench. People show their emotions sometimes.'

Mourinho, who had all but danced across the pitch after what was a great evening and victory, said after he hugged Frank and the team, 'We are in the quarter-finals and we have beaten the team who are, according to the press, the best in the world.

'Any result that put us through would have been fantastic. We faced a very good team, we were losing 2–1 before the start and we were without some of our best attacking players [the injured Arjen Robben and suspended Didier Drogba]. The way the players did it in the second half was fantastic.

'We scored four and should have scored six or seven. Barca could have had three, four or five.

'The football was magnificent. But over the 180 minutes I think the best team goes through. Until the last second, if they scored we were out. It was a game full of emotion.'

Frank's West Ham work ethic was evident a fortnight later, on 26 March, when he appeared for England against

Northern Ireland. His Chelsea colleague Joe Cole got the headlines but Frank helped him make them with a top rate performance. He was dominant throughout the match, set up Michael Owen's goal and got his reward with a goal from his deflected shot in the 62nd minute. 'My main aim is to keep shooting because if you don't you won't get that stroke of luck.

'Scoring goals is a big part of my game. I get tired at times in games but if you are an experienced player you can save your legs for a period and then come back strong again. I used to bomb forward at West Ham and get in the box all the time, but I've matured and I've learned the right time.

'At Chelsea we don't panic if we don't score in the first half. Facing defensive teams is not easy and you might dominate games but it's not necessary to score six in the first half.'

His goal against Northern Ireland – his eighth for England in 31 games – put him alongside World Cup winner Alan Ball, who won 72 caps, and Glen Hoddle, who was awarded 53. His performances for England in March 2005 also won him plaudits from the sport's most influential figures, and headlines like 'Lampard Joins The Elite' and 'Winning Ethos Drives On Tireless Lampard'.

The 4–0 England victory at Old Trafford had followed a day's shopping in Manchester. Given the afternoon off by Sven-Goran Eriksson, Frank, John Terry and David Beckham took their gold and black heavyweight credit cards to the High Street in Manchester. The next day the *Sunday Times* published a 'Young List' of the richest footballers in England, aged under 30. Frank Lampard and John Terry were positioned at joint number nine, each with a fortune of £8 million. So why shouldn't they be smiling?

They were easily spotted in their England 'sweats' but

while David Beckham arranged for the Adidas store to close to the public for three-quarters of an hour so he could browse in privacy – inevitably attracting the usual frenzied crowds that followed the England captain everywhere – Frank and John Terry and their shopping packages were winging their way through the Saturday afternoon shoppers.

19

In the final days of the 2004-05 season, Frank Lampard strode on, an assured, commanding figure on and off the pitch. He belted in the second goal when Chelsea triumphed over Fulham 3–1 in their London derby on 23 April.

That Saturday, it was 50 years to the day since Chelsea had last won the title and they were within one result of repeating that achievement with their 26th win in 34 League games. If Arsenal, in second place, failed to defeat Spurs 48 hours later then the title was theirs. Although Arsène Wenger conceded that Chelsea were 'very worthy' Premiership champions, his team denied them early official celebrations. Chelsea had waited half a century – and they would have to wait a little longer.

Jose Mourinho knew that his team had no doubts of their stature and said after the Fulham game, 'They were magnificent and at the end they felt they deserved to be champions.'

Sir Alex Ferguson suggested it had been over for Manchester United from the start, right from their first game at Stamford Bridge, which they lost 1–0 on 15 August 2004. 'We never caught up with Chelsea after that. This season is the first I can remember where I have to look at the first game and say that was *the* title decider.'

Months later, yes, the players did a lap of honour at

Stamford Bridge after that Fulham encounter and, given Chelsea's 14 point lead, you had to be a rather anal statistician to say they'd jumped the gun. All that was left was a rubber stamp, two points, and that was pretty certain away to Bolton Wanderers on 30 April. A long time since 23 April 1955, when they beat Sheffield Wednesday at home to win their only previous League title, and Roy Bentley was the captain. Bentley was present, as guest of honour, for the Fulham game and took a bow at half-time.

There's a long legacy to Chelsea, which Frank Lampard appreciates. He's grown up with football, with all its beauty and its cruelty. In the dwindling days of the 2005 season, at arguably the most golden moment in the club's history, there was an extravagant excitement to being such a high-profile Chelsea star. Yet he remained cool and calm – even after the monumental Champions League semi-final match at home to Liverpool.

Following the high drama of the Barcelona duel, there was more to come against the club they had beaten in the League Cup Final. They had a red carpet rolled out down the tunnel at Stamford Bridge that Wednesday evening, 27 April 2005; it was called the 'Road to Istanbul', where one of the English clubs would meet AC Milan in the richly anticipated final. In the biggest game of the domestic season, Jose Mourinho coached his team to play, ironically, not with a Continental passion but more of a stiff upper lip. They mustn't concede an away goal. But neither did they score. At Anfield, Liverpool would prove equally tight at the back, having sneaked a fourth minute lead with a hotly disputed goal from Luis Garcia.

The disappointment of missing out on the Champions League Final again was soon washed away. For most Chelsea fans, the Premiership was the one they wanted most, and they only had to wait three days to get it. Frank scored twice and completed his 4,570th minute of action as Chelsea took the title at Bolton's Reebok stadium, with three matches to spare. It was Chelsea's 27th win in 35 League games since the opening day when they beat Manchester United at Stamford Bridge. Frank starred in every game, his double at Bolton taking his goals for his most magnificent season to 18.

Commentators immediately singled out the English duo of Frank and John Terry as the basis for the glory. Yet Frank himself, elated at scoring the goals that sealed the title, said, 'This championship was not about a few individuals winning but the whole squad, management and backroom staff.'

The inspiration may have come from their Continental superstar coach Jose Mourinho, and the finances from Russia, but that reaction was the cool understatement of an Englishman.

The East End boy did good, very good, up the West End.

*   *   *

A year later, as World Cup fever heightened in 2006, Frank was being called 'Lampard the Legend'. After the England v Argentina encounter in November 2005, Alan Shearer described him as 'a world-class player'. Certainly his manager had no doubts. 'He is a complete player. He is very strong in every aspect. I wouldn't swap him for any player: Ronaldinho, Kaka or Andriy Shevchenko. He plays every game if it rains or snows. Away or home, soft or difficult opponents, whether they play a zonal system against him or are aggressive. He is my perfect player and I wouldn't change him for anyone.'

Praise indeed! But being perfect does have its handicaps. If you don't deliver perfection every time, then the doom watchers snarl that you've lost your touch. Also, in Frank's case, his expectations, as well as those of his fans, go forever skywards.

At the start of 2006, he had an astonishing year to look back on: he had set a Premiership record on 26 November 2005, when he walked out against Portsmouth at Fratton Park for his 160th consecutive league appearance. His record-breaking run of 164 consecutive matches ended when Chelsea beat Manchester City 1–0 (courtesy of a Joe Cole goal) on 28 December 2005. A virus stopped his incredible sequence just 10 minutes before the start of the game.

Mourinho revealed Frank's determination to play. 'Frank was feeling bad during the day. He wanted to play but during the warm-up he realised it was impossible. It was a big test for the players to play without him. But the answer of the team was magnificent. People talk about the power of money but I don't agree. This is the power of a group, the power of a group of friends, human beings playing together.'

Yet Frank's consistency set him apart from all others. His goal scoring, readiness to fight injury and cool temperament made him the ultimate gladiator. Frank tried to play down his achievement when it became apparent he would beat David James's total of 159 consecutive games, but Mourinho said that his 'perfect player' had had it in his sights for some time. With two games to go to the end of the 2004-05 season and Chelsea already champions, Lampard could have opted for early surgery on his toe. But he played on through the pain and reaped his accolades at Portsmouth. Mourinho said, 'He preferred to do it after games against Manchester United and Newcastle and carry on.'

Despite Frank's determination his manager was not

concerned about how much he would help England in the World Cup. A combination of occasional rest in less vital games and a month-long gap before the start of the tournament meant Frank would be on top of his game in Germany. 'He is a player who can recover well. He is very strong physically. Training with Chelsea is controlled and that means he can play a hard season in England... I think also he will have a good World Cup.'

At the end of 2005, Frank was voted second in the FIFA World Player of the Year poll, with only Ronaldinho rated above him; the same result was returned for the Ballon d'Or, Europe's top award. At the start of 2006, the England fans awarded him their Player of the Year trophy. Add the Premiership crown, the Carling Cup, the Football Writers' Player of the Year, a record for consecutive Premier League appearances and qualification for the World Cup as top scorer and you understand where 'Lampard the Legend' came from. He played 63 games and scored 28 goals in 2005. Always one for high standards, he thought he should have done better. 'I want more. I need to get my head down and keep trying to improve. I was very pleased. I wouldn't say I can't believe it because I've always strived to get to the very top, but it was a fantastic year for the club and the biggest prize was for the team in winning the League.

'England qualifying for the World Cup was a big thing for me. I didn't play in the last one and so to be a big part in getting us there and to know that we will be playing in the finals was a great end to the campaign for me.

'The one thing which rates above all of those, however, was the birth of my daughter Luna. Seeing her every morning – her smile – nothing on the football pitch can match that and it was the year's crowning moment for me.

'A baby gives you something extra in your life. It's a great change, the best change you can have, and it's nice to have a bit more perspective. Because of her, I don't come home and beat myself up after a bad game, as I would have done a few years ago.

'Football is an obsession. It's always in the back of your mind and, if I lived alone, I would probably sit around watching football on TV all the time. I always understood that there was more to life than football, but it's much easier when you come home to a little smiley face.'

Yet even if he had his little girl Luna – Spanish for 'moon' – to be obsessed about as well as football, Lampard insisted that in 2006 the burning ambition of everyone at Stamford Bridge was to become only the second team to win the Premiership in consecutive years. There seemed to be an understanding that Chelsea felt they must dominate English football in the way that Manchester United had, during their eight titles in the Premiership era, to convince people of their true greatness.

'We didn't set out to win one title and fade away or just win back-to-backs, but to win more and more in English football. You have to give ultimate respect to United, who managed to do that while Arsenal, despite their title successes, didn't. We will try very hard to win consecutive titles and we are hungry to go after that.

'Only when you have won one title and know what it takes can you understand how great an achievement it was for United to win so many. We aspire to be what Liverpool were in the seventies and eighties and what Manchester United have been for the past 10 years. That means not just winning the title two years on the trot, but doing it over the next five to ten years.

'In the second year, it is much harder because everyone lifts their performances against you, and not only opposing players but also the fans are more up for it. If anything goes wrong, people jump on it and say, "Is this the big blip?"

There are a lot of things on and off the pitch that you have to be even stronger to cope with after you win the first championship, and United became the best at that. They had success for 10 years, winning it back-to-back a few times. We are becoming accustomed to the demands more and more.

'Of course, I want to win the League but we want to win the Champions League and avenge the two semi-finals which we lost [to Monaco and Liverpool]. It sounds greedy to even talk about it, but yes I have aspirations to win them all.'

Looking ahead to the World Cup, he said, 'I believe in our team both individually and collectively. I think that we can go to Germany and do well. People talk about me being the most improved player and perhaps that is simply because I just want to get better, year after year.'

It was true: no player had shown greater determination to improve his game, fitness, leadership skills and image. Frank had made a terrific personal journey from being a figure of some fun for West Ham fans to one of world football's greatest stars. And one of the most admired. He gave an astonishing performance when he was named Footballer of the Year by the Football Writers' Association. One guest pointed out, 'A speech was required. In the same situation, Eric Cantona once honoured us with 30 seconds. Lampard treated us to more like 30 minutes of graciousness and gratitude.

'He thanked all his old coaches, his family and friends who had helped him to this point. He treasured the award, he said, because it was not just about playing ability, but also about how a player carried and conducted himself.

'There was even humour. Gordon Strachan had earlier passed on a question from his wife to Lampard: "How did you get rid of that fat arse?" "Tell her to come back on the first day of pre-season training and she'll be able to see it again," he replied.'

20

Frank's work for the Teenage Cancer Trust, which he has undertaken quietly but intently, has won him amazing admiration. In November 2005 he was one of the hosts, with Roger Daltrey of The Who and the designer Karen Millen, of a fundraising evening at Old Billingsgate in London. Frank worked the room like an Oscar nominee; there was time for everyone as he introduced his fiancée Elen Rives. He seemed nervous but happy to be there.

'Frank Lampard's Evening for Teenage Cancer Trust' followed his visit to see two teenage Chelsea fans, brothers both diagnosed with lymphoma. On another occasion, Frank took 11-year-old Lucy Hilton on to the pitch when Chelsea were presented with the Premiership trophy. Her brain tumour killed her only a few days later.

The distinguished sports writer Paul Hayward said in the *Daily Mail* on 23 November 2005, 'There is not a famous person in Britain who could have loaded more compassion into a speech about this truly evil disease and how it steals life from the young. Lampard played one of the great games of his life. It came 24 hours after he had made his 159th consecutive Premiership appearance.

'Off the pitch and on it, this son of old East End footballing stock has developed into a statesman, philanthropist and inspiration. Many of us went to Old Billingsgate on the banks of the Thames thinking John

Terry is Chelsea's leading candidate to succeed David Beckham as England captain. We left acknowledging a more powerful truth about Lampard's ability to see beyond the white lines of a football field.

'No slight is intended against Terry, who cheekily bid £13,000 for a day at Arsenal's training ground and pressed the flesh all night. But if either of them can teach young disciples of the game that you can be a caring member of society as well as a billboard god, then it's surely the man about to reach 160 not out.'

The Teenage Cancer Trust was, and is, raising funds for special units – each one costs £1.5 million – for young cancer sufferers. They look like the Big Brother house, have pool tables and cable television and most importantly are making a 15 per cent difference to recovery rates. The Trust said they were thrilled and proud to have Frank as one of their ambassadors.

He took no credit for helping raise more than half a million pounds at Old Billingsgate. He did, however, celebrate the birth of his daughter Luna. On 24 August 2005, five days after she was born, Frank scored the opener (Chelsea 4 West Bromwich Albion 0), his 50th Chelsea goal, and a baby-rocking celebration followed.

Elen Rives opted for a Caesarean birth. She particularly wanted her grandmother, aged 93, who was on holiday from Barcelona, to see the baby, and Frank explained, 'It was planned around that rather than around football.'

Luna Coco Patricia (for Frank's mother) Lampard was born at the Portland Hospital in West London, where David and Victoria Beckham's sons Brooklyn and Romeo were born. She then returned to her parents' £8.4 million house in Chelsea and to their French mastiff, Daphne.

A couple of months after his daughter was born, Frank explained his daily routine. 'Breakfast is usually a

mug of strong English Breakfast tea and a bowl of Coco
Pops. If I get bored, the Frosties come out. But I always
go back to Coco Pops – I've been having them since I was
a kid.

'We get the *Sun*, *Mirror* and *Daily Mail* delivered, so I
usually have a quick flick through and then set off in the
car – a blue Aston Martin – for the training ground in
Cobham. I'll turn on the radio or listen to music. I like U2
and Coldplay.

'There are days when it's harder to motivate yourself –
you're tired or have things on your mind, but on the whole
I enjoy it. I'm a bit of fitness fanatic anyway. I got that from
my father.

'I wanted to be a footballer for as long as I can
remember. It was all I thought about. But right from the
start dad drummed it into me that, as well as practice, you
had to be fit. Training lasts about an hour and a half, then
it's in the shower and lunch.'

Frank eats at the grounds, enjoying pastas, salads, meat,
chicken and fish. He's not fussy about food but eats up his
carbs a couple of days before games for extra energy.

'In the afternoon, mum often pops round for a cup of
tea. She and dad have bought a place in London, which is
great, and also means they're at all the games. I'm very
close to mum – a real mummy's boy, to be honest. We're
very similar. Quite sensitive and quite shy. Whereas dad's
been the big influence on my career, mum's been the one
who shaped me as a person: you know, behaviour,
manners, that kind of thing. These days she juggles a lot of
her time between me and my two older sisters, as they've
also got little girls.'

'Before bed, I'll let the dog out, do the lights, the alarm
and then I might read for a while. Sometimes, when I think
about all those dreams I had as a kid and where I am now,

I have to pinch myself. The hard work, the determination, the sacrifices – they all paid off ... Life right now couldn't be sweeter,'

But times, as Chelsea were to discover, do change.

21

Forty years on from England's World Cup victory, it was Germany who hosted the tournament. The result was not so good for either country. The expectations of Frank – player of the year for two years running – from the fans and media, were huge. But though he played every moment of every England game the team lost to Portugal on penalties in the quarter-finals. For the rising star of the global show, defeat in the tournament marked the start of a poor run of English form.

There were moments for Frank: he scored the only goal in a 2–1 defeat in a friendly with Germany, but England fans who had expected so much of him on the international stage were even frustrated enough to boo him at a few fixtures. Once again, he overcame the abuse from the disenchanted the only way he knows how – he regained his form.

It didn't happen overnight, and although Frank can be quite insular during bad periods, he retains the ability to get on with what he has to do in order to come through even stronger. Fortunately his Chelsea form wasn't suffering – it improved once again, for the fifth year running. His 16 goals in 2005-06 set a Premier League record for a midfielder. Chelsea won the League for the second time and, with John Terry out of consideration due to his back injury, Frank became captain for much of the following season.

The responsibility made him even better and he prospered under Mourinho, as did the club in general. When Chelsea won the 2007 FA Cup, beating Manchester United 1–0, it meant that Mourinho (and Frank) had taken every domestic trophy.

There was more bliss for Frank, and just as he became an FA Cup winner for the second time, Elen gave birth to a second daughter, Isla, a few hours after he lifted the trophy in front of jubilant Chelsea fans at the new Wembley Stadium. It was a memorable tournament for him in every way. In the third round of the Cup, on 6 January 2007, Frank had scored his first hat-trick for Chelsea against Macclesfield Town making him the FA Cup player-of-the-round.

But success didn't heal the problems between Mourinho and Abramovich. The stories of their unconventional working relationship suggested that Frank's mentor would go, but Mourinho insisted he'd only leave Stamford Bridge if he was carried out in a box, fired, or did not have his contract renewed in 2010. Behind the scenes, the tensions between owner and manager intensified.

The arrival of Avram Grant as Director of Football – against Mourhino's vibrant objections – did little to smooth things out. Grant got a seat on the Chelsea board and became part of the decision-making process. Then the Russian striker Andriy Shevchenko, Ambramovich's favourite, was bought though Mourinho was reluctant to play him because he wasn't scoring goals.

Frank kept his head down. There was clearly a lot of player support for Mourinho but, on 20 September 2007, the flamboyant figure who'd set London and football fans on fire with his antics and pronouncements, departed by 'mutual consent'.

For Frank and the team it heralded a big change. Avram

Grant became the new coach, but he failed to win any trophies during his year in charge despite going close. Chelsea finished runners-up in the Champions League, Premier League and League Cup.

Frank suffered from injury through the entire season and played his fewest games in years. Yet, on 16 February 2008, in a 3–1 fifth-round Cup win against Huddersfield, he became the eighth Chelsea player to score 100 goals for the club. He played to the crowd, stripping off his strip top to reveal a shirt emblazoned: '100 Not Out, They Are All For You, Thanks.'

After the FA Cup win, Frank announced he wanted to stay with Chelsea forever, yet it had been an unsettled season at Stamford Bridge. There were even rumours he wanted to join Mourinho wherever his old manager went. Professionally, it was a rough time for him but worse was to come.

Frank's mother Pat was taken to hospital in April 2008 with severe pneumonia. She was already extremely poorly and, as he and his family kept a bedside vigil, she seemed to be making a recovery. Things, he said, had brightened. 'Slowly, slowly she is coming through. I'm lucky to have a very tough mum. It's been a positive few days after a very difficult week.'

He was encouraged enough to leave her bedside for a Tuesday night Champions League semi-final against Liverpool on 23 April 2008, believing she was stable and on the mend. After the game, the self-confessed 'mummy's boy' said, 'This time last week it was very bleak. I won't go into the details but we were getting a very bleak outlook. That was the hardest moment for me and my family in my life.'

All looked OK and, after the 1–1 draw at Anfield, Frank was able to joke, 'She would have a right go at me for not playing this game.' Suddenly, however, her condition deteriorated. Frank was told his mother might not pull through, and she was put on a life support system. He maintained a bedside vigil.

On 24 April Chelsea made a statement. 'Everybody at Chelsea Football Club is absolutely devastated to hear the tragic news of the passing away of Pat Lampard, Frank's mother. Our sincerest and deepest condolences go out to Frank, his father Frank Snr, sisters Natalie and Claire and to their immediate family and friends.

'Pat was a very familiar face to many people at Chelsea FC. Her unswerving support for her son's career was evident at virtually every game that Frank participated in; regardless of where it was being played, she would always be there to watch him with Frank's dad.'

Because of the wide-ranging concern for Frank's wellbeing, his agent Steve Kutner gave a statement reassuring fans that he was OK. 'Frank would like to acknowledge and say thank you for the compassion shown to him by the manager Avram Grant and all the staff at Chelsea Football Club during what has been a terribly traumatic period for him and his family. Frank and his family would also like to thank all the people who have been inundating them with wishes of support.'

Few in the crowd will forget Frank's appearance on 30 April in the second leg of Chelsea's Championship League semi-final against Liverpool.

Liverpool went out 4–3 on aggregate, but only after Frank took a penalty in the 98th minute of extra time. Everyone felt for him. Was it too much pressure for him? Should he be allowed to? Fans at Stamford Bridge and watching on television had their hands to their mouths. Some looked away. How would he feel if he missed?

He scored with panache and, as he ran from the spot, he

looked up at the sky, as if at his mother. And from then on, Frank raised his eyes to the heavens whenever he scored. Which is precisely what happened in the final against Manchester United on 21 May 2008, when he equalized a moment before half-time sending the match into extra-time. Chelsea eventually lost 6–5 on penalties, but later Frank was elected UEFA Club Midfielder of the Year.

For Abramovich finishing second best, especially in Moscow, wasn't good enough. He wanted trophies and, when Grant was sacked a few days later, there was no pretence about 'mutual consent'.

And how did all this affect Frank? He had adapted to the differences between Grant and Mourinho and now he had to learn again: this time from Luiz Felipe Scolari. Things were set to change again under the man known as Big Phil. What didn't and never changed was Frank's astonishing physical soundness and determination to be a winner with Chelsea and England.

22

Luiz Felipe Scolari arrrived on 1 July 2008 at Stamford Bridge with impressive credentials, becoming the first World Cup winning boss to manage a Premiership club. He got off to a glowing start and bought in (for £8 million) Deco, whom he knew from running the Portuguese national team. Despite tempting offers from the Brazilian, Robinho stayed out of bounds at Real Madrid. On 13 August 2008, Frank signed a five-year contract with Chelsea in a £39.2 million deal, which made him the then-highest paid Premiership player.

He kept his employer happy with goals galore, including his 150th for Chelsea and a chip shot from 20 yards against Hull City, which had Scolari in raptures, saying, 'It was the best goal I have seen; only a player with his intelligence could have done that.'

Frank was used to praise for his goals from midfield, so this left-footed, delicate chip – not a power shot from out of the box – was remarkable.

On 17 January 2009, Frank made his 400th Chelsea appearance against Stoke City, scoring the last minute winner. Despite the accolades and awards for his work on the pitch – including being named Chelsea Player of the Year three times – not everything was easy. He and Elen, who had been together for seven years, were having problems in their relationship.

There were the gossip column headlines and, finally, Frank confirmed that he and his fiancée had parted by putting their £8 million town home, a six-bedroom, six-bathroom Georgian house near Stamford Bridge, on the market. The couple had moved there from Surrey, but not long after they had settled in, the house had been burgled in an early morning raid. As part of his £1 million improvements to the property, Frank introduced elaborate security measures.

There were countless stories about the break-up of the relationship, some as wide of the mark as the £15 million divorce settlement. The true figure was much more conservative, both parties agreed that it should remain private and Luna and Isla's financial futures were assured.

This was followed by another upset at work. Scolari took Chelsea to some impressive wins, but his first defeat – Liverpool won 1–0 on 26 October 2008 at the Bridge – ended the record of 86 home wins, an impressive figure which had lasted more than four years. This proved to be a bad omen.

Chelsea were defeated at Manchester United, then beaten at home by Liverpool and Arsenal, were knocked out of the League Cup by Burnley and drew in the FA Cup against Southend United.

Scolari, a World Cup winner with Brazil in 2002, was given his marching orders on 9 February 2009, with Chelsea proclaiming, 'The results and performances of the team appeared to be deteriorating at a key time in the season.'

Scolari had been in charge for just seven months. It was a personal decision by Abramovich, who feared his team would lose to Juventus in the last 16 of the Champions League. The owner went to his club's Cobham training ground and Scolari was gone in a moment.

The cigar-chomping Dutchman Guus Hiddink arrived to do a little moonlighting, because he was still managing the Russian national team at the time. In his caretaker role,

Hiddink endeared himself to the team and the fans. His first game was a 1–0 away victory against Aston Villa. Back at the Bridge, it was the same score against Juventus in the Champions League, which brought a rare public smile to Abramovich's face.

It seemed that by going Dutch, Chelsea were on a winner, and they followed this up with a 3–1 Champions League win against Liverpool at Anfield, but the coming Champions League semi-finals were both controversial and demoralising. Frank adopted a mature view of what was to most people a disgrace. He gave his view, but did so with characteristic calm.

On 6 May 2009 at Stamford Bridge, Chelsea were knocked out of the competition by Barcelona through a 93rd-minute Andres Iniesta strike, making the score 1–1. The away goal rule won the semi-final clash for the competition's eventual winners.

But it was not Iniesta's goal that angered the players and fans – and neutrals. It was the Norwegian referee Tom Henning Ovrebo who cruelly deprived Chelsea of a place in the Champions League final. Chelsea fervently believed they had at least four good penalty calls during the match. All were ignored. John Terry had a go at Ovrebo but it was Didier Drogba who got the headlines when he ran on to the pitch to confront him at the final whistle. Drogba, who had been substituted after 72 minutes, had to be restrained as Ovrebo went down the tunnel.

John Terry defended the reactions of the Chelsea players and Drogba in particular. 'I am fully behind Didier for the way he reacted. The man wants to win. You can see the passion that he played with during the game and the passion afterwards.

'People are saying we shouldn't have reacted the way we did but the fact is that six decisions went against us in front of 40,000 people. And for the ref to not give one of them is unusual.'

Frank added, 'The penalties are clear as day. The linesman's in line, the referee's nearby. There were about three of them that were clear as anything and I can't understand why they weren't given.'

His midfield partner Michael Ballack, who was booked for running 40 yards alongside Ovrebo to protest when the fourth penalty appeal was rejected, said, 'Everybody saw it and it was not one or two decisions, there were at least three, four or five we can discuss.'

Guus Hiddink supported his players. 'I can fully understand it in the emotion of the game, as long as they don't touch him... It's not just one decision in doubt but several... and I protect my players for this when they have this emotion ... with loads of energy and adrenalin in their bodies.'

Although a bitter moment, that evening was no reflection on Hiddink's achievements at Chelsea. He only had one other loss while in charge, 1–0 to Spurs at White Hart Lane. In the final home game of the season (when Chelsea beat Blackburn Rovers 2–0), his name was the chant of the day with cries of, 'Sign him up.' Frank joined John Terry and other players in calling for the caretaker manager to stay, but Hiddink was true to his word and returned full-time to the Russians.

Enter Carlo Ancelotti. Viva Italia? Or possibly a problem for Frank?

23

Another Italian was managing Frank's fortunes at international level. Fabio Capello took charge of England in 2007, following the failure to qualify for Euro 2008, and has so far had a massive impact on the team. Frank hit top form, having taken on a more defensive, deeper role. But at club level there were teething pains with Ancelotti. Frank seemed squeezed out of the scoring with just one goal in 10 games.

Yet as Ancelotti worked his system, his Chelsea team were playing out of their skins towards the end of 2009, with Frank's confidence flourishing as he built on his England glories. He'd scored his first international goal in two years in a 4–0 win over Slovakia in March 2009.

The following month, on the anniversary of his mother's death, he became embroiled in a row with James O'Brien of LBC radio, in London. It followed reports of Elen Rives and his daughters having to live in a small flat while he was enjoying a lavish lifestyle. She allegedly said that he had turned their family home into a bachelor pad while she was struggling to raise their daughters. O'Brien added that men who allow their children to live in inferior circumstances to them were weak and scum.

Frank, unsurprisingly, responded in no uncertain terms. He wasn't having it, especially that he was a bad father: 'Since I've had kids, every penny I earn and every yard I run on the football pitch is for my kids. It hurts me every day when I wake up and my kids are not there.'

Frank told O'Brien he was an 'idiot' for upsetting his family on the first anniversary of his mother's death and said of Elen: 'Someone approached her in a bar and got her talking after she had a few drinks. My ex-girlfriend is very distressed about the story. She gave it away in a moment of weakness.'

In a 15-minute rebuttal of the allegations, Lampard said: 'My sister just phoned me up because she was upset about you calling me scum. Did you call me that? [Luna and Isla] are living in a temporary flat which is actually in Fulham. It's not a bad flat at all. I am buying [them] a house at the moment which is going to be of equal standard to mine if not better.

'Luckily I have a relationship with my ex-girlfriend where we will share custody or whatever you want to call it. For three nights a week – and I'm away two or three nights for my football – the kids wake up in my house. I look after them solely.

'Let me tell you something now, right, my mother died a year ago today and that has had a huge impact on my life and my family's life and on my sister's life, and unfortunately that has had a huge impact on my relationship at home. I find it insulting that you insinuate I wouldn't fight tooth and nail for my kids. You don't know anything about me.

'I have to wake up and listen to idiots like you say, "I read this, this is what he's doing" and it's wrong. I put up with it and keep my mouth shut. The only reason I rang you is because my sister is distressed and as I said, it's the anniversary of my mum's death. Do you think my sister needs to hear idiots like you saying that on the radio station?'

O'Brien subsequently apologised for bringing up the

issue on the anniversary of Pat Lampard's death. Frank received overwhelming calls of support.

Despite his ongoing distress at the loss of his mother and separation from his daughters, Frank remained a contained, true professional. Chelsea won the Community Shield, beating Manchester United on penalties. Then Frank was on the score sheet with Deco and Ballack in a win against Sunderland on 19 August 2009.

But Chelsea crisis headlines appeared after they lost 3–1 to Wigan and followed up with a poor 1–0 away win over Apoel Nicosia in the Champions League. Was it Ancelotti's midfield diamond that was hampering Chelsea, and not bringing out the best in Frank?

Frank said, 'I don't know why people say we're not clicking. We lost against Wigan and we didn't play well there at all. Yet if you look over the season, we have clicked together as a team. We try to win every game and when we don't we just try harder in the next match.'

While the critics waited for Frank to fire on all cylinders for Chelsea under Ancelotti, the words of a rather good football manager echoed around the Chelsea and England hero. In an unprecedented tribute to an opposing player, Sir Alex Ferguson raved, 'Frank Lampard is an exceptional player – a huge asset to Chelsea. You pay attention to players who can get goals from midfield and he's been averaging 20 a season. You don't see him getting into stupid tackles or making a habit of becoming involved in silly rows. He stayed restrained in the middle of all that bother after Chelsea were knocked out of the Champions League by Barcelona and made a point of swapping shirts with Iniesta. As I say, Lampard is exceptional!'

Frank certainly was exceptional during England's defeat of Croatia in a victory which sent them on their way to South Africa and the 2010 World Cup finals.

He desperately wanted to bring that trophy home to England. As did all the team. With the memory that their opponents denied them a place at Euro 2008 (when England lost 3–2 at Wembley), they were fired up before the Croatia game. Frank said of being knocked out of the Austria-Switzerland tournament, 'It was a very low point for all of us, individually and as a group. We won't forget that and will use it as a positive. We need to keep cool heads, keep calm, but also show passion and desire to win the game. There certainly won't be tackles anyone is pulling out of.

'The spirit is much more enhanced these days. I've never known the team so confident going into games, wanting to win them and waiting for the next game. We are certainly not lacking in any spirit and we are calmer these days as well.'

Frank rubbished allegations by the Croatian coach Slaven Bilic, a former team-mate of his at West Ham, that England were 'missing some Englishness' – missing some fighting spirit, that is – under Capello.

Frank reckoned Bilic was playing mind games. 'He's very intelligent, almost in the way Jose Mourinho was at Chelsea. He's always thinking one step ahead and thinking of any edge he can get. The important thing is not to get sucked into that. We know we have improved a lot, but we are not the finished article.

'England fans respond to constant effort. Everyone in their England career has slight ups and downs. David Beckham is probably the ideal story. Sometimes he has had stick, but now he is the hero and quite rightly so because he keeps coming back and giving his all.

'I think it's modern culture. It's unfortunate, but as players we have to take it like it is. I had a little bit of it. Ashley Cole has. The only benefit is that people will come out stronger. It makes you tougher. You get the adulation that comes with playing for England, which is probably superior to anything else. So there are two sides of the coin.

'With England now it's more disciplined; it's good to see a manager come in and be upset. If you didn't see that it could translate to the players. A lot of things have happened to me in my career with England and Chelsea and whenever it's backs against the wall, for whatever reason, it brings a togetherness.'

Togetherness or not, Frank opened the scoring against Croatia with a penalty in the seventh minute. His team's 5–1 routing of the opposition was sweet revenge and inspired Capello to observe, 'We played, for me, the best 20 minutes of the qualification games. The first 20 minutes were fantastic, we passed the ball quickly, the quality of the passes was very, very good. The play was sharp in every moment, both when we had the ball and when we didn't.

'The first target is reached. We had to get to South Africa. Expectation is always high but we have to play to win because we are England. Why not? All the players in the squad who have been selected are really good. We are one of the best teams in the world who can play against all the teams out there. We have always to play with the spirit we played with this evening.'

For Frank it was a great relief to be back on such a hopeful, gleaming, golden road. 'We've put the record straight to some extent. We've put in nothing but hard work, the confidence has come on.

'This is the first step. It's fantastic. We're very level headed in the squad. We've been through our lows in the last few years, so we know what it's all about. I am enjoying my football again for England and I am playing in a team that's got such work rate and quality in it. I just want to keep enjoying it and keep going. There's still work to be done and a long way to go but it's nice to be enjoying it at the moment and to get excited.

'Hopefully we will make a bigger impact in the World Cup than last time. It was disappointing to get knocked out at the stage we did. I think with the way we are playing makes this the best England team I have been involved with. I have never been in an England team that has won so many qualifying games and so well. I have been in good teams before but the way we are playing at the moment is brilliant.'

POSTSCRIPT

'**B**rilliant' was also how the new decade was looking for Frank and Chelsea. As it began, Frank Lampard's champion fan remained Sir Alex Ferguson. At a glance, his generosity seems surprising, but the wily Scot is an admirer of talent and hard work.

Frank might be an imposing weapon against his Manchester United, but Sir Alex has been around long enough to witness many players – and managers – steer their careers like kamikaze pilots. As such, he has huge respect for the high flyers who don't self-destruct on the flamboyance of fame.

Frank had become even more of a legendary Chelsea hero by November 2009 when United met Chelsea at the Bridge for a pivotal encounter. It had been a wobbly run-up at first with successive Premier League away losses at Wigan and Aston Villa, and the usual rumours over whether Roman Abramovich still thought Ancelotti had the 'X' factor.

There were also serious questions about the dressing room and Frank and the team provided rapid-fire answers: four games, four wins, 17 goals scored and not one conceded. The talk about poor set-piece defending stopped. The narrow midfield dictated by Ancelotti? Suddenly, nothing could be more effective. The critics were silenced.

After the away defeats and the bounce-back, Ancelotti

said, 'We accepted this criticism because the first thing we had was self-criticism. This is normal when we don't do well, it is important to improve. And I think this team has improved very well. At this moment, we are doing very, very well.'

When Chelsea tormented Blackburn 5–0, Frank had put on a vintage display and got two goals. The match also saw Joe Cole's first League start for 10 months, and his impact and popular return left Frank feeling bad that he had taken the penalty for Chelsea's fourth goal, when he could have given it to his friend.

Frank then led the way with a first-half penalty in Chelsea's relentless drive to the title with their 4–0 win over Bolton. But what brought most gasps from the crowd was his ferocious 30-yard shot in the second half that had the crossbar twanging – it looked like it was dancing in the wind. And then his cute back heel enabled Didier Drogba to get Chelsea's fourth in added time.

But the giant contribution in championship terms was the wonderful free kick which led to John Terry's header, which nicked Nicolas Anelka on its way to the back of Manchester United's net on Sunday 9 November 2009, the day Chelsea went five points clear. With their arms around each other after the goal, Frank and John Terry, fists clenched, were sending out only one signal: catch us if you can!

The win certainly gave the Blues the edge for the Premier League crown. It also validated Alex Ferguson's faith in Frank. Although he was furious with referee Martin Atkinson's decision to award a free kick after Darren Fletcher's challenge on Ashley Cole, maybe he could console himself with the fact that Frank took it. Controversial or not, the goal did the job and it didn't change the view that Sir Alex offered before the game. 'I think Chelsea are using their experience really well. Frank

Lampard has retained that fantastic energy to get down the pitch and you would have to say that his record in terms of appearances is quite exceptional for a midfield player. He's 31, but he obviously looks after himself to get that kind of playing record. They've got an exceptional player there.'

And certainly one that the owner is as pleased with as he is with the Chelsea style of football.

Roman Abramovich says he wants to win games with his team playing exciting football. It's a combination endorsed by Ron Gourlay, who took over in 2009 as the club's chief executive. 'Over the next five years we've got to shoot for the stars. With no disrespect to the competition, which is an incredibly high standard, I'd still like to think we can win the Champions League twice in the next five years. That may sound aggressive but I think we can do it.

'We're competing for every competition we enter and for the success of the football club, you have to win trophies consistently. You can't win the Premier League one year and slip away for three years. You've got to be pushing every time.'

Which is the only way Frank Lampard knows – the heroic way.